This book belongs to:

Table of Contents

Table of Contents

Consonant Blends

1 Fill in the blank with the correct consonant blend from the word bank below.

bring	clock	crafts	drum	flag
plant	scooter	skunk	spider	stick

a) We raised the _______________ during the school assembly.

b) Can you _______________ me a glass of water, please?

c) I saw a _______________ crawling up the wall.

d) My friend rode her _______________ down the hill with a big smile.

e) I used a _______________ to draw in the sand at the beach.

f) The _______________ chimed at midnight.

g) The musician played a rhythm on the _______________.

h) My mom has a beautiful _______________ on the windowsill.

i) Be careful around a _______________! They can spray a smelly liquid.

j) In art class, we made _______________ by folding and cutting paper.

Consonant Blends (cont.)

2 Complete the word search. Circle the words as you find them.

S	Q	Y	B	T	V	D	E	L
W	A	U	G	R	A	S	S	F
A	N	T	O	U	F	X	P	E
N	G	Y	E	C	R	H	A	Q
B	L	A	N	K	E	T	C	W
V	O	F	R	E	S	H	E	N
J	V	U	E	P	C	L	A	P
O	E	Z	D	S	M	E	L	L

Words to search for:

blanket
clap
fresh
glove
grass
smell
space
swan
truck

3 Unscramble the consonant blend word.

a) nrgee g___ ___ ___ ___

b) cksna s___ ___ ___ ___

c) ptlae p___ ___ ___ ___

d) pnis s___ ___ ___

e) ickrt t___ ___ ___ ___

f) lwonc c___ ___ ___ ___

4 Fill in the blank with the correct consonant blend.

a)

______ug

b)

______ame

c)

______onge

Long Vowel Patterns

1 The letters ***ai, ay, ee, ea, ie, igh, oa, ow, ue,*** and ***ui*** are vowel patterns. Fill in the missing vowel pattern for the word.

a)

sn______l

b)

cr______

c)

b______ch

d)

spr______

e)

j______ce

f)

c______t

g)

l______f

h)

d______

i)

b______l

j)

l______t

k)

tiss______

l)

sh______p

Long Vowel Patterns (cont.)

2 The letters ***ai, ay, ee, ea, ie, igh, oa, ow, ue,*** and ***ui*** are vowel patterns. Fill in the missing vowel pattern for the word.

a)

b_____ver

b)

s_____p

c)
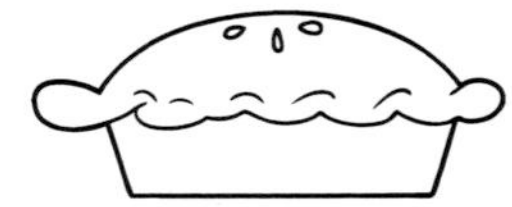
p_____

d)

sn_____

e)

qu_____n

f)

p_____nt

g)

h_____

h)

kn_____t

i)
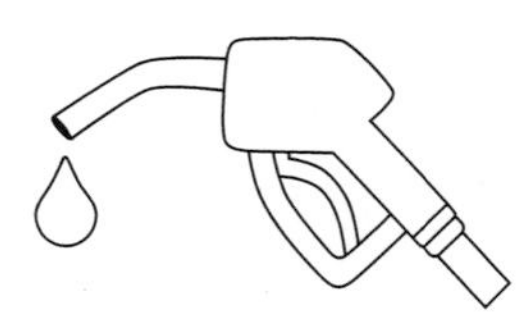
f_____l

j)

sw_____p

k)

fr_____t

l)
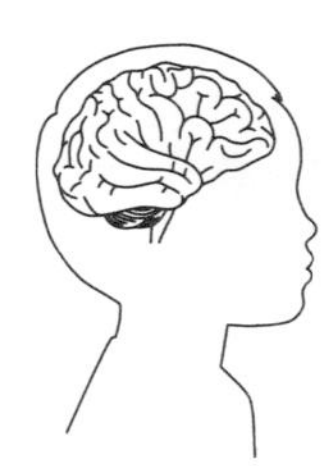
br_____n

Long Vowel Patterns (cont.)

3 The letters ***ai, ay, ee, ea, ie, igh, oa, ow, ue,*** and ***ui*** are vowel patterns. Fill in the missing vowel pattern for the word.

a) 

tr______

b) 

cl______

c) 

s______t

d) 

t______

e) 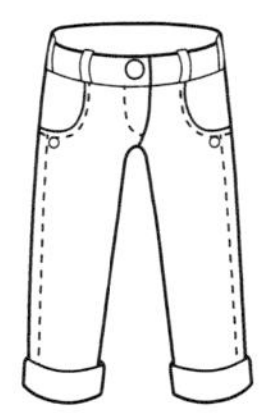

j______ns

f) 

ch______n

g) 

b______

h) 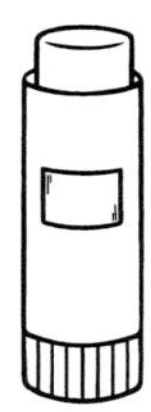

gl______

i) 

n______t

j) 

g______t

k) 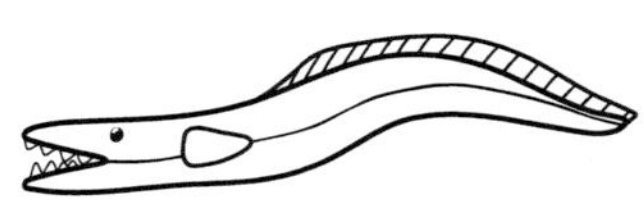

______l

l) 

r______n

R-controlled Vowels

The letters ***ar, er, ir, or,*** and ***ur*** are r-controlled vowels.
Fill in the missing r-controlled vowel for the word.

1

sk____t

2

wat____

3

f____k

4

sh____k

5

y____n

6

t____tle

7

f____n

8

b____d

9
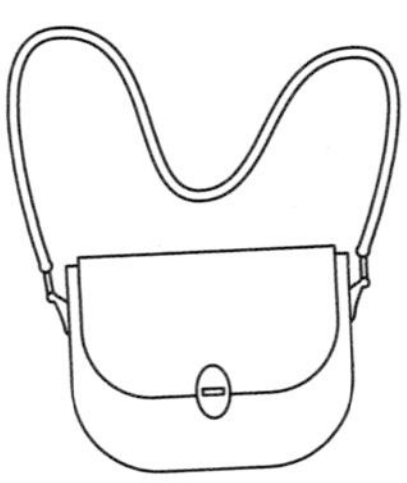
p____se

10

h____se

11

j____

12

ladd____

Unit 1

What Is a Noun?

A **noun** is a word that names a **person**, **place**, or **thing**.

1. Circle the nouns that name a **person**.

   Elias   run   boy   pretty   man   Amy   mother   throw   doctor

2. Circle the nouns that name a **place**.

   school   library   kitchen   walk   winter   mall   beach   Canada

3. Circle the nouns that name a **thing**.

   say   bottle   ruler   running   ask   yell   socks   leaf   frog

4. Circle all the **nouns** in the group of words.

   a) pen   dance   apple   bedroom   softly

   b) small   teacher   smiled   couch   rough

   c) dog   shout   brother   shiny   backyard

5. Circle the **nouns** in the sentence.

   a) The basement is very dark.

   b) Juliette walked to the house slowly.

   c) The car drove past our school.

6. Write a sentence that has three nouns.

   ____

Make a Noun Collage

Cut out pictures from magazines and flyers that represent nouns.
Paste them below to make a collage.

What Are Proper Nouns?

A **proper noun** names a specific person, place, or thing.
A **proper noun** begins with a capital letter.

For example:

- Names of **people** or **pets.**
- Specific places, such as a **country, province, city,** or **town.**
- Names of **holidays.**
- Names of **days of the week** and **months of the year.**

1 Use a proper noun to complete the sentence.

a) I would like to visit the province of ______________________________.

b) The first day in March is ______________________________.

c) Toronto and ____________________ are Canadian cities.

d) ______________________________ was my teacher in Grade 2.

e) My favourite day of the week is ______________________________.

2 Write two proper nouns.

_________________________ _________________________

Making Nouns Plural

To make many **nouns** plural, just add the letter ***s***.

rock ☞ *rocks* *window* ☞ *windows* *flower* ☞ *flowers*

For some nouns, you need to do something different.

Nouns ending with...	To make the noun plural...
s, ***x***, ***ch***, or ***sh***	Add ***es*** *one fox – two foxes*
consonant + ***y***	Change the ***y*** to ***i*** and add ***es*** *one fly — two flies*

Use the **plural** of the **noun** below to complete the sentence. Use each noun only once. Choose a noun that makes sense in sentence.

bush	**dish**	**fox**	**puppy**	**wish**

1. After dinner, I helped wash the ______________________.

2. My friend adopted two ______________________ from the animal shelter.

3. My mother planted four ______________________ in the backyard.

4. I saw two ______________________ in the forest.

5. In the fairy tale, the girl got to make three ______________________.

Tricky Plural Nouns

For some nouns that end with **o**, add the letters ***es***.
For other nouns that end with **o**, just add the letter ***s***.

Add *es*	**Add *s***	
echo – echoes	*patio – patios*	*video – videos*
hero – heroes	*photo – photos*	*zero – zeros*
potato – potatoes	*piano – pianos*	
tomato – tomatoes	*radio – radios*	

1 Complete the sentence by writing a **plural noun** from the lists above.

a) We printed the ______________ that we took on our vacation.

b) My mom made mashed ________________ for dinner.

c) The _________________ in our garden look bright red and ripe.

d) I enjoy playing duets with my sister on our __________________.

2 Rewrite the sentence below to make the underlined nouns **plural**.
Do not use the words ***a*** or ***an*** before a plural noun.

a) The <u>hero</u> heard an <u>echo</u> in the canyon.

____

b) Larry sent me a <u>video</u> of a <u>potato</u> from his garden.

____

Tricky Plural Nouns (cont.)

For most nouns that end with ***f***, change the ***f*** to a ***v*** and add ***es***.
For a few nouns that end with ***f***, just add the letter ***s***.

Change *f* to *v* and add *es*		**Just add *s***
elf – elves	*scarf – scarves*	*chef – chefs*
half – halves	*shelf – shelves*	*cliff – cliffs*
leaf – leaves	*thief – thieves*	*roof – roofs*
loaf – loaves	*wolf – wolves*	*sheriff – sheriffs*

3 Complete the sentence by writing a **plural noun** from the lists above.

a) We shared the cookie by cutting it into two ________________.

b) I have many ________________ to keep me warm during winter.

c) Three ________________ howled loudly during the night.

d) The library has many ________________ full of books.

4 Rewrite the sentence below to make the underlined nouns **plural**.
Do not use the words ***a*** or ***an*** before a plural noun.

a) The <u>sheriff</u> stops the <u>thief</u> from stealing.

____

b) A <u>leaf</u> blew over the <u>cliff</u>.

____

Tricky Plural Nouns (cont.)

For nouns ending with the letters ***fe***, change the ***f*** to a ***v*** and add ***s***.

knife – knives   *life – lives*   *wife – wives*

5 Change the noun ending in ***f*** to ***v*** and add ***s*** to make it **plural**.

a) elf ____________________   b) half ____________________

c) wolf ____________________   d) loaf ____________________

e) leaf ____________________   f) shelf ____________________

g) knife ____________________   h) life ____________________

Some **nouns** use a new word to name **more than one**.

foot ⟶ ***feet***

6 Draw a line to match the word with the word that names **more than one**.

child ●	● mice
mouse ●	● people
person ●	● children

Nouns Review

1 Circle all the **nouns** in the group of words.

a) table jump tree dog gently

b) big doctor laughed pink mall

c) house yell sister dull beach

2 Use a proper noun to complete the sentence.

a) I would like to visit the country of ______________________.

b) My favourite holiday is ______________________.

c) The name of my street is ______________.

3 Write the plural of the noun.

a) knife ______________ b) brush ______________

c) baby ______________ d) photo ______________

e) book ______________ f) foot ______________

g) person ______________ h) box ______________

i) leaf ______________ j) puppy ______________

Unit 2

Singular Possessive Nouns

A **possessive noun** shows who or what something belongs to.

Add an **apostrophe** (') + ***s*** to a **singular noun** to show belonging.

Singular Noun	Possessive Noun	Example Sentence
Anne	*Anne**'s***	***Anne's** new glasses look nice.*
dog	*dog**'s***	*The **dog's** paws are muddy.*
car	*car**'s***	*The **car's** horn is very loud!*

1 Write the **singular possessive noun** for the example below.

a) the boots that belong to Julie _______________ boots

b) the bed that belongs to the dog the _______________ bed

c) the stickers that belong to Wyatt _______________ stickers

d) the car that belongs to the man the _______________ car

2 Rewrite the sentence. Use a **singular possessive noun** to replace the underlined words in the sentence.

Example: He painted the legs <u>of the table</u>.
*He painted the **table's** legs.*

a) The treats <u>of the dog</u> are in the jar.

____

b) The front <u>of the car</u> is dented.

____

More Practice with Possessive Nouns

Rewrite the sentence. Use a **singular possessive noun**.
Look at the examples below.

Examples: The handle of the cup is broken.
The cup's handle is broken.

I like the kitten that belongs to Tim.
I like Tim's kitten.

1. The zipper of my jacket is broken.

____

2. Please give me the address of the museum.

____

3. Did you find the shoe that belongs to Amy?

____

4. The roar of the lion is loud!

____

5. The chair that belongs to the school is in the hallway.

____

6. This is the apron that belongs to my grandmother.

____

Plural Possessive Nouns

How do you change a **plural noun** into a **possessive** noun?

If the **plural** noun ends with an ***s***, add an **apostrophe** (′).

If the **plural** noun does **not** end with an ***s***, add an **apostrophe** (′) + ***s***.

Plural Noun	Possessive Noun	Example Sentence
sisters	*sisters'*	*My **sisters'** shoes got wet in the rain.*
children	*children's*	*The **children's** parents are coming.*

Write the **plural possessive noun** for the example below

1. the cats that belong to my brothers — my ________________ cats
2. the pool that belongs to my aunts — my ________________ pool
3. the chirping of the birds — the ________________ chirping
4. the howls of the dogs — the ________________ howls
5. the singing of the people — the ________________ singing
6. the books belonging to the men — the ________________ books

Some **plural nouns** do not end with ***s***.

children women men people

Add an **apostrophe** (′) + ***s*** to turn these plural nouns into **plural possessive nouns.** *Examples: children's women's men's people's*

Possessive Nouns Review

1 Write the **singular possessive noun** for the example below.

a) the shoes that belong to Amy ____________ shoes

b) the bed that belongs to the cat the ____________ bed

2 Write the **plural possessive noun** for the example below.

a) the laughter of the children the ____________ laughter

b) the toy that belongs to my cousin my ____________ toy

3 Rewrite the sentence. Use a **plural possessive noun**.

a) The tools <u>that belong to the men</u> are in the tool box.

____

b) The enclosures <u>of the animals</u> are very large.

____

c) The houses <u>that belong to the people</u> are on this street.

____

d) The games <u>that belong to my brothers</u> are on the shelf.

____

Unit 3 Pronouns for People

A **pronoun** is a word that takes the place of one or more nouns.
Use these pronouns to take the place of nouns that name **people**.

I you he she we they him her them us

1. Use a **pronoun** to take the place of the underlined word or words.

a) Amelia likes cats.

______________ likes cats.

b) The boys played soccer.

______________ played soccer.

c) Bao shared the pizza with Austin and Mya.

Bao shared the pizza with ______________.

2. Rewrite the sentence. Change the underlined word or words to a **pronoun**.

a) Troy ran in the field with the class.

____

b) Sofie gave the book to Lucas.

____

c) My aunt and uncle hugged my brother and me.

____

Pronouns for Things

A **pronoun** is a word that takes the place of one or more nouns.

Pronouns take the place of nouns that name **people, places,** or **things.**

Use the pronouns below to take the place of nouns that name **things.**

it they them

1 Use a **pronoun** to take the place of the words in brackets.

a) John was writing in ______________. (the notebook)

b) ______________ are growing in the garden. (the flowers)

c) I found ______________ under the table. (my pencils)

d) ______________ are handmade by grandma. (the sweaters)

2 Rewrite the sentence to use pronouns for **people** and **things**. Change the underlined word or words to a **pronoun**.

a) <u>The teachers</u> gave <u>the sheet of paper</u> to <u>Lee and Amy</u>.

____

b) <u>The tomatoes</u> are too small for <u>Moe and Omar</u> to pick.

____

c) <u>Rebecca and Billy</u> gave <u>those Christmas presents</u> to <u>Jack and me</u>.

____

Possessive Pronouns

A **possessive pronoun** is a word that shows something belongs to a person, place, or thing. It tells us without naming that person, place, or thing, like when you say "my toy" or "her book" or "its streets" or "its fur."

Use a **possessive pronoun** before a noun.

my your his her its our their

1. Circle the **possessive pronoun**. Remember that a possessive pronoun shows who or what something belongs to.

   a) Stacey said, "It is cold outside, where is my hat?"

   b) His house is the red one.

   c) The two cats ran to their bowl for dinner.

   d) "Is your birthday this month?" asked Mr. Chang.

   e) My cousin and I wash our hands before we eat lunch.

   f) The dog wagged its tail when I walked through the door.

2. Write a sentence using a **possessive pronoun**.

Possessive Pronouns (cont.)

3 Rewrite the sentence. Replace the underlined **possessive noun** with a **possessive pronoun**.

a) Jason watched <u>Jason's</u> favourite movie.

____

b) We are going over to <u>Melissa's</u> house to swim.

____

c) The Smiths went to the store in <u>the Smiths'</u> car.

____

d) <u>The bed's</u> sheets need to be changed.

____

e) "Yazan, is it <u>Yazan's</u> turn to play the game?" Luca asked.

____

f) The doctors said, "It is <u>the doctors'</u> job to help you feel better."

____

g) Trudy said, "You can have <u>Trudy's</u> last cookie."

____

More Possessive Pronouns

Sometimes, **possessive pronouns** do **not** come before a noun.

Examples: This book is mine. *This book is yours.*
This book is his. *This book is hers.*
This book is ours. *This book is theirs.*

Mine is a **possessive pronoun** that takes the place of *my book.*

The possessive pronouns below **do not** have to come before a noun.

mine yours his hers ours theirs

1. Underline the **possessive pronoun** that comes **before** a noun. Circle the **possessive pronoun** that **does not** come before a noun.

   a) I asked Pedro if this is his backpack. He said, "It is not mine."

   b) Fatima finished cleaning her room, but Romeo is still cleaning his.

   c) Sally and Leo said a cat was sleeping on their porch. "That cat is not ours," they said.

2. Fill in the blank to complete the sentence. Use the words in the learning box to help you.

   a) The red bike belongs to Sara. It is ______________.

   b) My sister and I baked a cake. It is ______________.

   c) We borrowed the neighbours' rake. It is ______________.

   d) I drew this picture for you. It is ______________.

Pronouns Review

1 Rewrite the sentence. Change the underlined word or words to a **pronoun**.

a) <u>The teacher and the principal</u> discussed the school's plans.

____

b) <u>Mirna</u> is going to the store to buy fruit for <u>Edwardo</u>.

____

c) <u>Nadia and Amy</u> said goodbye to <u>my parents and me</u>.

____

2 Use a **pronoun** to take the place of the words in brackets.

a) Anthony said he is bringing ____________. (the present)

b) ____________ are done baking in the oven. (the cookies)

c) Can you put ____________ in the drawer? (the socks)

3 Underline the **possessive pronoun** that come **before** a noun.
Circle the **possessive pronoun** that **does not** come before a noun.

a) Jack found his book on the table. He said, "There it is!"

b) The cat chased its tail in circles, but the dog did not chase his.

c) Mrs. Campbell's class finished watching their movie, but we did not finish watching ours.

Unit 4

What Is an Adjective?

An **adjective** is a word that describes a noun.

A big lion ran after me!

The word *big* is an **adjective**. It describes the noun *lion*.

1 Circle the **adjective** in the sentence. Underline the **noun** it describes.

a) The tall tree was filled with fruit.

b) Mr. Chung had a huge smile on his face.

c) She received a lovely gift from her friend.

d) We watched a funny movie last night.

e) My grandfather has a big garden at the back of his house.

f) He bought a fresh apple from the store.

g) We found a tiny kitten in our backyard.

h) She put on a beautiful dress for the party.

i) A small bird built its nest on our balcony.

j) Mrs. Rodriguez gave us a difficult puzzle to solve.

k) We played with the bouncy ball in the park.

l) They are going on a long trip next month.

m) We adopted a cute puppy from the shelter.

n) I found a shiny coin under the bed.

What Is an Adjective? (cont.)

2. In the sentence below, write an **adjective** that makes sense. Underline the **noun** your adjective describes.

a) I have a ________________________ backpack.

b) My new sweater is very ________________________.

c) Elyssa told me a ________________________ story.

d) A ________________________ runner will win the race.

e) Dad put the ________________________ flowers in a vase.

f) The ________________________ cat chased a mouse.

3. Circle the **adjective** in brackets that fits best.

a) He put the (dirty   yellow) clothes in the washing machine.

b) She found a (loud   silver) necklace in the drawer.

c) The (worst   kind) woman helped me find my way.

d) My little brother loves to read (scary   favourite) stories.

e) The teacher was impressed by his (noisy   neat) handwriting.

f) The (little   purple) kitten was very (difficult   playful).

Adjectives Before Nouns and After Nouns

Sometimes an adjective comes **before** the noun it describes.

*We walked across the **shiny** floor.*

Sometimes the adjective comes **after** the noun.

*The floor was **shiny**.*

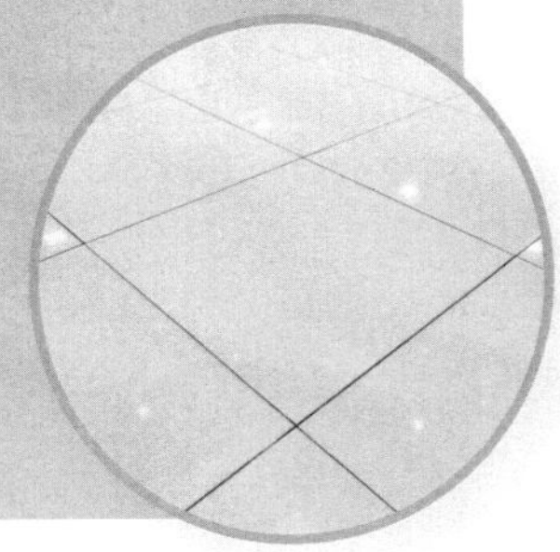

1 Circle the **adjective** in the sentence. Underline the **noun** it describes.

a) The stars in the sky look so tiny from here.

b) We had an amazing dinner at grandma's house.

c) The forest at night can be a little scary.

d) Do you think the homework is easy?

e) Jaime watched that funny movie.

f) We hiked along the challenging trail we hiked.

g) My mom baked bread and it smells delicious.

2 Circle the **adjectives** and underline the **nouns** in the sentence. Draw an arrow from the adjective to the noun it describes.

a) The water in the blue lake feels refreshing.

b) The children were happy when the pink flowers bloomed.

c) An old man fed the noisy birds at the park.

Adjectives Can Describe How Many

Numbers can be adjectives.

I popped ***three*** *balloons!*

Three is an **adjective** that describes the noun ***balloons***.

Some **adjectives** do not tell exactly how many.

I have ***some*** *questions for you.*

Some is an **adjective** that describes the noun *questions.*

1 Circle the **adjectives** that describe the **nouns**.

a) We have two cats at home.

b) The school library has five computers.

c) We counted eight birds sitting on the telephone wire.

d) The recipe calls for two cups of flour and one teaspoon of salt.

e) The soccer team scored four goals in the first half of the game.

2 Unscramble the adjectives using the word box.

all	few	many	most	several	some

a) alevres ________________

b) ynam ________________

c) wfe ________________

d) emos ________________

e) toms ________________

f) lla ________________

Using Adjectives to Compare Two Things

Use a **comparative adjective** for comparing two people or things.

Use a **superlative adjective** for comparing one person or thing with a group of other people or things.

The turtle is **big.**

The zebra is **bigger.**

The hippo is the **biggest.**

Fill in the chart.

	Root Word	Comparative (er)	Superlative (est)
1	nice		
2		stronger	
3			richest
4	dark		
5	calm		
6		quicker	

Adjectives That Compare More Than Two Things

1 Use the **adjective** in brackets to complete the sentence. Use the correct form of the adjective to compare **more than two things**.

a) The spaceship is the ____________________ toy in the toy store. (cool)

b) The sunflower is the ____________________ flower in the garden. (tall)

2 Use the **adjective** below the line to compare **more than two things**. Remember to write ***the*** before an adjective that ends with ***est.***

a) The cheetah is ____________________ land animal in the world.
fast

b) The firetruck is ____________________ vehicle on the street.
loud

c) The ocean is ____________________ body of water on Earth.
largest

For adjectives that have **two** syllables and **end with *y***, change the ***y*** to ***i*** and add ***er*** or ***est*** when you want to compare.

shiny ☞ *shinier* ☞ *shiniest*   *easy* ☞ *easier* ☞ *easiest*

3 Choose the correct word to fill in the blank.

a) These are the ____________________ flowers I've ever seen.
prettier   prettiest

b) Jack has the ____________________ dog in our neighbourhood.
shaggier   shaggiest

Tricky Adjectives That Compare

Watch out for these tricky adjectives that compare!

Adjective	To Compare Two Things	To Compare Three or More Things
good	*better*	*best*
bad	*worse*	*worst*
far	*farther*	*farthest*
many	*more*	*most*

Use the **adjective** below the line to complete the first sentence in the pair. Then circle the correct answer in the second sentence. Write ***the*** before an adjective that compares **more than two things.**

1. The chocolate cake tasted ________________ than the vanilla cake.
   good

   This sentence compares (two things   more than two things).

2. The traffic here is ________________ than in the neighbouring town.
   bad

   This sentence compares (two things   more than two things).

3. Of all my classes, math is ________________ challenging.
   many

   This sentence compares (two things   more than two things).

4. Of all my friends, Sarah lives ________________ from my house.
   far

   This sentence compares (two things   more than two things).

Adjectives That Use *More* and *Most* to Compare

Some adjectives compare by using the words ***more*** and ***most***.

Use the word ***more*** with adjectives to compare **two things**.

Use ***the most*** with adjectives to compare **three or more things**.

1 Use the correct form of the word in brackets to compare.
Remember to use ***the*** with words ending in ***est***.

a) The sun is ______________________ object in the sky.
bright

b) This game is ______________________ than the one we played last time.
fun

2 Fill in the blanks with the correct form of ***more*** or ***the most***.

a) This puzzle is ______________ challenging than the one we did yesterday.

b) John is ______________ athletic student in our school.

c) Ice is ______________ slippery to walk on than snow.

d) That was ______________ exciting movie I have ever seen.

e) The new mall is ______________ crowded than the old one.

f) He is ______________ successful author in our country.

g) The roses are ______________ beautiful flowers in the garden.

h) My younger brother is ______________ energetic than me.

Adjective Noun Poem

1 Fill in the chart with **adjectives** that describe your noun of choice.

My poem is about ______________________________

Colour	**Size**
Shape	**Texture**
Number	**Sound**

Poem Checklist

- ☐ I used an adjective to describe colour.
- ☐ I used an adjective to describe shape.
- ☐ I used an adjective to describe number.
- ☐ I used an adjective to describe size.
- ☐ I used an adjective to describe texture.
- ☐ I used an adjective to describe sound.

Adjective Noun Poem (cont.)

2 Use your **adjectives** that describe your noun to fill in the poem. Decorate your poem.

______________________________!

__________, __________, __________,
noun noun noun

__________ __________,
adjective noun

__________ __________,
adjective noun

__________ __________,
adjective noun

These adjectives describe a __________!
noun

__________ __________,
adjective noun

And __________ __________, too,
adjective noun

__________, __________, __________,
adjective adjective noun

Just to name a few!

I love __________ __________!
adjective noun

Using the Articles *A*, *An*, and *The*

Use ***an*** with singular nouns beginning with a vowel sound.
Example: an orange shirt

Use ***a*** with singular nouns beginning with a consonant sound.
Example: a happy child

Use ***the*** with specific singular and plural nouns.
Example: the fast dog

Write the correct word (***a, an***, or ***the***) in the sentence.

1. She is ____________ best student in our class.

2. Can you please give me ____________ large piece of paper?

3. There is ____________ egg in the robin's nest.

4. We are going to visit ____________ CN Tower during our trip.

5. Daniel asked for ____________ glass of water.

6. There is ____________ apple tree in our garden.

7. I found ____________ old book in ____________ attic.

Adjectives Review

1 In the sentence below, write an **adjective** that makes sense. Underline the **noun** your adjective describes.

a) I have a ______________________ car.

b) My new sweater is very ______________________.

c) The ______________________ puppy wagged its tail.

d) The ______________________ apple tasted ______________________.

2 Circle the **adjective** that describes the **noun**.

a) I have two brothers and one sister.

b) The gym has many basketballs.

3 Use the correct form of the word below the line to compare. Remember to use ***the*** with words ending in ***est***.

a) Hussein is ____________________________ than his sister.
tall

b) Anna is ______________________________ person I know.
friendly

4 Write the correct word (***a, an***, or ***the***) in the sentence.

a) She is _______ fastest runner in the class.

b) My mom bought me ______ ice cream cone.

c) I saw ______ bird flying in the sky.

Unit 5

What Is a Verb?

A **verb** is a word that tells what someone or something is doing.

Karen reaches for the book. *The dog barks at the squirrel.*

1 Circle the **verb** in each sentence.

a) I eat a sandwich for lunch.

b) We play soccer on Sundays.

c) Jackson ties his shoelaces.

d) The woman knits a sweater.

e) In winter, we build a snowman in our backyard.

f) On his birthday, John excitedly opens his presents.

2 Circle the all the **verbs** in each group of words.

a) studies bed yells butterfly blows

b) washes marker paper forest watches

c) paints fixes school cars sings

d) doors nets listens reads flower

e) drives food explores mittens sends

Verb Poem

1 A **verb poem** describes an action and does not rhyme.

Verb poems have only three lines.

Line 1 is three verbs.
Line 2 is three more verbs.
Line 3 is a sentence that the verbs are describing.

For example:

Run, bounce, dodge

Jump, shoot, score

We won the basketball game!

Write your own verb poem about a topic.

____

____

____

Try writing another verb poem with different verbs!

____

____

____

Verbs: Choosing the Correct Action

Some **verbs** have similar meanings.

Choose the right verb so that people know what you are saying.

Here are verbs that have similar meanings:

Throw, toss, hurl

Call, yell, shout

Eat, snack, nibble

Like, love, adore

Run, sprint, jog

Choose the correct **verb** for each of the following sentences.

1. My family ____________________ dinner at 6:00. (eats/snacks)

2. Sometimes I ____________________ when I get angry. (call/yell)

3. Can you please ____________________ me the ball? (toss/hurl)

4. I really ____________________ my grandma. (like/love)

5. In gym class, we ____________________ lightly around the field. (jog/sprint)

The Verbs *Be*, *Do*, and *Have*

Here are the **present tense** forms of the verbs ***be***, ***do***, and ***have***.

Be	Do	Have
*I **am***	*I **do***	*I **have***
*he **is**, she **is**, it **is***	*he **does**, she **does**, it **does***	*he **has**, she **has**, it **has***
*we **are**, you **are**, they **are***	*we **do**, you **do**, they **do***	*we **have**, you **have**, they **have***

1. Write the correct **present tense** form of the verb ***be***.

a) We ______________ playing a fun game at recess.

b) She ______________ explaining a new lesson to the students.

2. Write the correct **present tense** form of the verb ***do***.

a) He _____________ the lawn raking with his dad in the fall.

b) I _____________ my homework every evening after school.

3. Write the correct **present tense** form of the verb ***have***.

a) You _______________ a new toy that I would like to play with.

b) She _______________ a big collection of colourful seashells.

The Verbs *Be*, *Do*, and *Have* (cont.)

Here are the **past tense** forms of the verbs ***be***, ***do***, and ***have***.

Be	Do	Have
I **was**, *he* **was**, *she* **was**, *it* **was**	*I* **did**, *he* **did**, *she* **did**, *it* **did**	*I* **had**, *he* **had**, *she* **had**, *it* **had**
we **were**, *you* **were**, *they* **were**	*we* **did**, *you* **did**, *they* **did**	*we* **had**, *you* **had**, *they* **had**

4 Circle the correct **past tense** form of the verb in brackets.

a) She (was were) a talented dancer.

b) We (do did) chores to help keep our house clean.

c) We (has had) a family movie night last Friday.

d) He (do did) his homework yesterday before bed.

e) You (was were) happy, and I (was were) sad.

5 Choose the correct verb (***be***, ***do***, or ***have***).
Then write the correct **past tense** form of the verb.

a) They ____________ marshmallows to roast when they went camping.

b) Yesterday, I ____________ my homework after school.

c) She ____________ happy when she received a surprise gift.

d) I ____________ a fantastic idea for a new art project last week.

e) They ____________ cold when they played in the snow without gloves.

More Practice with *Be*, *Do*, and *Have*

Review the **present tense** and **past tense** forms of the verbs ***be***, ***do***, and ***have***.

Present Tense

	Be	Do	Have
I	*am*	*do*	*have*
he, she, it	*is*	*does*	*has*
we, you, they	*are*	*do*	*have*

Past Tense

	Be	Do	Have
I, he, she, it	*was*	*did*	*had*
we, you, they	*were*	*did*	*had*

1 Look at the **verb** in bold. Is it in the **present tense** or **past tense**? Circle your answer, then **check** the charts above to see if your answer is correct.

a) They **were** excited when they went to the concert. **present past**

b) He **is** a musician and plays in a band. **present past**

c) They **had** a meal at the new restaurant in town. **present past**

d) She **did** what she could to help her friend in need. **present past**

e) It **has** a lock on it to keep people out. **present past**

f) Do you think you **are** ready for the test? **present past**

g) She **was** the winner of the singing competition. **present past**

More Practice with *Be*, *Do*, and *Have* (cont.)

2 Read the sentence and decide whether it needs a **present tense** or **past tense** verb. Then write the **correct form** of the verb in brackets.

a) Yesterday, she ___________ surprised when it started to rain. (be)

b) You ___________ a great sense of humour. (have)

c) He ___________ not enjoy the movie last night. (do)

d) We ___________ excited about our upcoming vacation. (be)

e) I ___________ interested in learning new languages. (be)

f) Do you ___________ any plans for the weekend? (have)

3 Read the sentence and decide whether it needs a **present tense verb** or a **past tense verb**. Write the **correct form** of the verb.

a) Last week, it _____________ very warm and sunny.

b) She _____________ a puzzle before her friend came over.

c) I _____________ a doctor's appointment tomorrow.

d) At the hockey game last night, we _____________ cheering for our team.

e) Last year, they _____________ a superhero themed birthday party.

f) He _____________ a science experiment, then finished his homework.

Linking Verbs

A **linking verb** is a verb that does **not** show **action**.

Use ***am*** when you are referring to yourself.

Use ***is*** when you are referring to one.

Use ***are*** when you are referring to more than one.

1. In the sentence below, a **verb** is in bold. If it is a **linking** verb, circle it. If it is an **action** verb, underline it.

   a) The dinosaurs at the museum **were** huge.

   b) The rabbit **hops** quickly in the garden.

   c) The sun **is** shining brightly in the sky.

   d) We **are** learning to ride a bicycle.

   e) The monkey **climbed** up the tree.

2. Find the **verbs** in the sentence below. Circle the **linking** verb. Underline the **action** verb.

   a) My little brother hid from the neighbour. He is shy.

   b) This playground is so big. Let us play some more.

   c) The talent show was amazing. We clapped a lot.

   d) These paintings are beautiful. An artist painted them.

   e) We rolled snowballs outside. The weather was very cold.

Spelling Present Tense Verbs

For most **present tense** verbs, add ***s*** if **he**, **she**, or **it** does the action.

For verbs that end in a **consonant + *y***, change the ***y*** to ***i*** and add ***es***.

I study – she studies *they carry – he carries*

For verbs that end with ***s***, ***x***, ***ch***, or ***sh***, add ***es***.

I kiss ☞ she kisses *I fix ☞ he fixes*

they pinch ☞ it pinches *you wish ☞ he wishes*

In the blank, write the correct **present tense** of the verb below the line.

1. The bird ________________ high in the sky.
   fly

2. My dog ________________ at the birds every day.
   bark

3. My grandpa ________________ us some hot cocoa on cold days.
   mix

4. At lunch, Leo always ________________ his sandwich.
   finish

5. My sister ________________ her nose when it is itchy.
   scratch

6. The soccer player ________________ the ball to her teammate.
   pass

7. When the baby ________________, it is usually because he is hungry.
   cry

8. Cassie ________________ the button at the light to cross the road.
   press

Past Tense Verbs

Past tense verbs tell what happened in the **past.**

Verb	Present Tense	Past Tense
talk	*Today, I talk.*	*Yesterday, I talked.*
	Today, she talks.	*Yesterday, she talked.*

For many verbs, add ***ed*** to the verb to make the past tense.
If the verb already ends with **e**, just add ***d***.

1 Write the **past tense** of the verb below.
Add ***ed*** or ***d*** to make the past tense.

a) jump ____________________ b) play ____________________

c) escape ____________________ d) talk ____________________

e) laugh ____________________ f) help ____________________

g) cook ____________________ h) cough ____________________

2 Complete the sentence. Write the **past tense** of the verb below the line to show that the action happened in the past.

a) We ____________________ the movie last night.
watch

b) I ____________________ in Ottawa for two years.
live

c) This morning, I ____________________ my teeth before school.
brush

Spelling Past Tense Verbs

For many verbs that end with **consonant + vowel + consonant**, double the final consonant before adding ***ed***.

hop ☞ *hopped* *clap* ☞ *clapped* *zip* ☞ *zipped*

For most verbs that end with a **consonant + *y***, change the ***y*** to an ***i*** and add ***ed***.

study ☞ *studied* *marry* ☞ *married*

1 Write the **past tense** of the verb below the line.
Double the final consonant before adding ***ed***.

a) We ________________ up the fruit for our salad.
chop

b) Grandma ________________ a cozy sweater for me.
knit

c) The train ________________ at the station to pick up passengers.
stop

2 Write the **past tense** of the verb below the line.

a) Dad ________________ crispy chicken for our family dinner.
fry

b) We ________________ our playroom and put away our toys.
tidy

c) I ________________ the picture from the book onto my paper.
copy

d) The chef ________________ to prepare the meal for the hungry customers.
hurry

Tricky Past Tense Verbs

The **past tense** of some verbs does not end with ***ed***.
Watch out for these tricky verbs when you use the past tense!

Present Tense	Past Tense
get, gets	*got*
give, gives	*gave*
have, has	*had*
say, says	*said*

Present Tense	Past Tense
come, comes	*came*
drive, drives	*drove*
eat, eats	*ate*
fall, falls	*fell*

1. Write the **past tense** of the verb below the line.

a) Last summer, we ________________ a delicious picnic in the park.
have

b) At lunch today, I ________________ a juicy apple.
eat

c) Grandma ________________ thank you for the gift.
say

d) She ________________ asleep on the cozy couch.
fall

2. Rewrite the sentence. Change the **past tense verb** to **present tense**.

a) He drove the toy train around the track.

____

b) We gave the dog a treat for behaving well.

____

Tricky Past Tense Verbs (cont.)

Watch out for these tricky verbs when you use the **past tense**!

Present Tense	Past Tense
buy, buys	*bought*
draw, draws	*drove*
drink, drinks	*drank*
find, finds	*found*

Present Tense	Past Tense
know, knows	*knew*
go, goes	*went*
take, takes	*took*
think, thinks	*thought*

3 Write the **past tense** of the verb below the line.

a) We ________________ to the park to play on the swings.
go

b) Malik ________________ a shiny seashell on the beach.
find

c) I ________________ a picture of a beautiful sunset.
take

d) Belinda ________________ of a creative idea for a project.
think

4 Rewrite the sentence. Change the **past tense verb** to **present tense**.

a) We knew the answer to the riddle.

____

b) I drank hot chocolate on a cold winter day.

____

Future Tense Verbs

Future tense verbs tell about things that will happen in the **future**.

To make future tense verbs, use the helping verb ***will***.

One Person or Thing	More Than One Person or Thing
I will walk	*We will walk*
You will walk	*You will walk*
He/She/It will walk	*They will walk*

1. Complete the sentence. Write the **future tense** of the verb below the line to show that the action will happen in the future.

a) During summer vacation, I ______________________ my grandparents.
visit

b) This weekend, they ______________________ a sandcastle.
build

c) Tomorrow, Jordan ______________________ his bike to school.
ride

d) In an hour, I ______________________ a song at the talent show.
sing

2. Rewrite the sentence. Change the **past tense verb** to a **future tense** verb.

a) We packed our bags for the family roadtrip.

____

b) He planted a vegetable garden in the backyard.

____

Helping Verbs: Present and Future Tenses

A **helping verb** is a special word that helps another verb in a sentence. It tells more about the action or state of the main verb.

The helping verb ***is*** helps us show something happening now:

I am excited. *He is eating.* *They are playing.*

1 Choose ***is***, ***am***, or ***are*** to fill in the blank.

a) My friends and I ____________ planning a surprise party for our teacher.

b) The cake ____________ in the oven.

c) I ____________ looking forward to our field trip next week.

d) The excited children on the bus ____________ singing loudly.

2 Read the sentence carefully. Identify the helping verb and main verb.

a) The students are learning a new topic.

Helping Verb: ______________ Main Verb: ___________________

b) I am eating my lunch at noon.

Helping Verb: ______________ Main Verb: ___________________

c) My little brother is riding his bike to school.

Helping Verb: ______________ Main Verb: ___________________

Helping Verbs: Present and Future Tenses (cont.)

Use the **helping verb *will*** to tell about things that will happen in the **future**.

*Tony **will** <u>clean</u> his room in a few minutes.*
*Samantha **will** <u>arrive</u> tomorrow afternoon.*

When you use ***will*** before a **main verb**, the main verb does **not** end with ***ing***.

3 Rewrite the sentence to make the action happen in the **future**. Use the helping verb ***will***.

Examples: The garbage truck is coming.
The garbage truck will come.

a) My parents are cooking dinner in the kitchen.

____

b) I am writing a letter to my friend.

____

c) The bus is picking us up at eight o'clock.

____

d) The students are cleaning up the classroom.

____

Helping Verbs: Past Tense

A **helping verb** helps the main verb to show an action. Use these helping verbs to tell about things that have **already happened**.

has had have was were

Below, the main verb is underlined, and the helping verb is in bold.

The rain **has** <u>stopped</u>.

My neighbour **had** <u>painted</u> her house.

The students **have** <u>made</u> signs for the sale.

He **was** <u>laughing</u> at the joke.

They **were** <u>eating</u> pizza.

1. Identify the helping verb to tell about an action that has already happened.

a) It has snowed heavily this winter. Helping Verb ________________

b) They had baked a pie for Grandma. Helping Verb ________________

c) He was building a tower with blocks. Helping Verb ________________

d) You have played soccer in the park. Helping Verb ________________

e) We were helping with the chores. Helping Verb ________________

2. Use each of these helping verbs in a sentence: ***was*** and ***were.***

____

____

Helping Verbs: Past Tense (cont.)

Use the **helping verbs *was*** and ***were*** to tell about things that have **already happened**.

Below, the **main verb** is underlined, and the **helping verb** is in bold.

> *My brother* ***was*** *<u>helping</u> Mom clean up.*
>
> *The flags* ***were*** *<u>flapping</u> in the wind.*

Was and ***were*** are used with **main verbs** that end with ***ing***.

3 Circle the correct **helping verb** in brackets to tell about an action that has already happened.

a) The robin was (build building built) a nest in the tree.

b) Last night, the stars were (shine shining shone) brightly in the sky.

c) He was (ride riding ridden) his bike in the park.

d) The students were (study studying studied) for their test.

4 Circle the correct **main verb** to use with the **helping verb** in the sentence.

a) Amelia was (skips skipped skipping) rope in the playground.

b) They were (watch watching watched) a movie last night.

c) He was (bake baking baked) brownies for dessert.

d) The students were (write writing wrote) letters to their friends.

Subject–Verb Agreement

The **subject** of a **verb** is the person, people, thing, or things doing the action. Below, the **subject** of the verb is in bold, and the **verb** is underlined.

The subject and verb in a sentence should match with each other in number. A singular subject will have a singular verb, and a plural subject will have a plural verb.

*The **child** <u>laughs</u> at the joke.* *The **children** <u>laugh</u> at the joke.*

1 Write the correct form of the **verb** below the line. Make sure the subject and the verb **agree**.

a) The cars ________________ down the road.
drive

b) Mason ________________ his homework after dinner.
finish

c) The fireflies ________________ in the dark.
glow

d) Ms. Abbas ________________ the students how to multiply.
teach

e) Our dog Prince ________________ when my mom sings.
howl

f) My little sisters ________________ to school every day.
skip

Subject–Verb Agreement (cont.)

2. Circle the correct **present tense** form of the verb to make the subject and verb **agree**.

a) My grandparents (bake bakes) cookies for me.

b) My plant (grow grows) in the springtime.

c) My dad (fix fixes) broken toys with his tools.

d) The students (run runs) around the track for the race.

e) The dolphins (jump jumps) out of the water.

3. Write the correct **present tense** form of the verb below the line to make the subject and verb **agree**.

a) The doctor ________________ our temperature at the clinic.
take

b) The chefs ________________ delicious meals in the restaurant.
cook

c) The firefighter ________________ to put out the fire.
rush

d) Mr. Reid ________________ the plants in the garden.
water

e) Stella ________________ her dog in the bathtub.
wash

Pronoun–Verb Agreement

The **subject** of a **verb** is the person, people, thing, or things doing the action.

Sometimes, the **subject** of a verb is a **pronoun**.
Below, the **pronoun** that is the **subject** of the verb is in bold, and the **verb** is underlined.

***He** <u>takes</u> the money off the table.*
***They** <u>give</u> the children some oranges.*

1 Write the correct form of the **verb** below the line. Make sure the subject and the verb **agree**.

a) I ________________ my favourite book before bedtime.
read

b) She ________________ her dance routine in the gym.
practice

c) He ________________ the flat tire on his bike.
fix

d) Our neighbours ________________ out good treats at Halloween.
give

e) They ________________ tiny blankets for their dolls.
knit

f) Tim ________________ a picture of his cat Fluffy.
paint

Pronoun–Verb Agreement (cont.)

2. Write the correct **present tense** form of the **verb** below the line to make the **subject** and **verb agree**.

a) She ________________ him a note after class.
pass

b) They ________________ fresh apples from the market.
buy

c) He ________________ different animals in his science book.
study

d) We ________________ a family of ducks in the pond.
notice

3. Circle the correct **present tense** form of the verb below the line to make the **pronoun subject** and the **verb agree**. Then see if you can answer the riddle.

a) It (keep keeps) you warm in bed on chilly nights. What is it? ________________

b) They (twinkle twinkles) in the sky at night. What are they? ________________

c) It (buzz buzzes) to wake you up in the morning. What is it? ________________

d) They (help helps) you to eat soup. What are they? ________________

e) It (go goes) around your waist to hold pants up. What is it? ________________

f) People (toast toasts) marshmallows over it. What is it? ________________

Verbs Review

1 Write the correct **present tense** form of the verb ***be***.

a) You ________ my best friend.

b) I ________ a student.

c) We ________ excited for the trip.

d) He ________ tall and strong.

2 Find the **verbs** in the sentence below. Circle the **linking** verb. Underline the **action** verb.

a) We are playing a game of tag in the backyard.

b) He is jogging in the park.

c) I baked a cake for Mom. The cake was delicious.

3 Write the **past tense** of the verb below. Add ***ed*** or ***d*** to make the past tense.

a) watch ____________________

b) close ____________________

c) bake ____________________

d) help ____________________

4 In the blank, write the correct **present tense** of the verb below the line.

a) We ________________ in the pool during summer.
swim

b) Carter ________________ his lines for the school play.
study

c) The neighbours' dog ________________ at the mailman.
bark

Verbs Review (cont.)

5 Rewrite the sentence to make the action happen in the **future**. Use the helping verb ***will***.

a) I am drawing a picture in my notebook.

____

b) They are watching a movie at the theatre.

____

6 Identify the **helping verb** to tell about an action that has already happened.

a) The chef has cooked a meal. Helping Verb ____________

b) They had finished their homework. Helping Verb ____________

7 Circle the correct **present tense** form of the verb to make the subject and verb **agree**.

a) The students (run runs) during recess.

b) The teacher (explain explains) a lesson to us.

8 Write the correct **present tense** form of the **verb** below the line to make the **subject** and **verb agree**.

a) They ____________________ their groceries from the store.
carry

b) Melody ____________________ her cat while she is at school.
miss

Unit 6 Adverbs Describe How or Where

An **adverb** describes a verb.

It describes **how, when**, **where,** or **how often** an action happens.

Tara quickly tied her shoes.

The adverb *quickly* describes **how** Tara tied her shoes.

1. Underline the **adverb** that tells **how** an action happens.

a) The baby bird hungrily chirped for its mother.

b) The snow falls gently from the sky.

c) Julian excitedly jumped into the pool.

d) The workers carefully built the roof.

An **adverb** describes a verb.

It describes **how, when**, **where,** or **how often** an action happens.

Eddie and Tyler look <u>outside</u>.

The adverb *outside* describes **where** Eddie and Tyler look.

2. Underline the adverb that tells **where** an action happens.

a) During the storm, the friends gathered inside.

b) The laughing children run around.

c) I accidentally dropped my pencil somewhere.

Adverbs Describe When

An **adverb** describes a verb.

It describes **how, when**, **where,** or **how often** an action happens.

Cathy will visit us <u>tomorrow</u>.

The adverb *tomorrow* describes **when** Cathy will visit.

1 Underline the adverb that tells **when** an action happens.

a) They playfully run around in the park on sunny days.

b) Jenny sometimes dances in her room.

c) I quickly finish my homework before dinner.

d) We excitedly visit the park on weekends.

e) They have soccer practice every Tuesday after school.

2 Underline the adverb that tells **when** an action happens.
Then complete the next sentence.

a) Soon, the snow will fall.

The adverb ___________ tells **when** the action __________ happens.

b) Our favourite show plays next.

The adverb ___________ tells **when** the action ____________ happens.

Adverbs Describe How Often

An **adverb** describes a verb.

It describes **how, when**, **where,** or **how often** an action happens.

They sometimes go camping in August.

The adverb **sometimes** describes **how often** they go camping in August.

These **adverbs** describe **how often** an action happens:

constantly (all the time)
frequently (very often)
usually (most of the time)
occasionally (once in a while)
seldom (not very often)
rarely (almost never)

1 Underline the adverb that tells **how often** an action happens.

a) He jumped on the trampoline twice.

b) Penny usually rides her bike to school.

c) Andre rarely forgets his lines in the school play.

2 In the **second** sentence, write one of the **adverbs** from the list above. Choose an adverb that **means the same** as the underlined words.

a) The lion roars very often. The lion ______________________ roars.

b) The puppy sleeps all the time. The puppy ______________________ sleeps.

c) I almost never eat candy. I ______________________ eat candy.

d) We smile most of the time. We ______________________ smile.

Adverbs Review

1. Underline the **adverb** that tells **how** an action happens.

   a) She slowly walked along the beach.

   b) The bird flew quickly into the tree.

   c) Our puppy barked excitedly when Dad came home.

2. Underline the adverb that tells **where** an action happens.

   a) We put the cookies inside the hot oven.

   b) The roses are blooming outside in the garden.

   c) The cat is sleeping over there on the shelf.

3. Underline the **adverb** that tells **when** an action happens.
   Then complete the next sentence.

   a) She reads a bedtime story at night.

   The adverb ___________ tells **when** the action ___________ happens.

   b) We will be riding our bikes today.

   The adverb ___________ tells **when** the action ____________ happens.

4. Underline the adverb that tells **how often** an action happens.

   a) He frequently visits his grandparents on weekends.

   b) They occasionally have ice cream as a treat.

Unit 7 Complete Subjects

There are two parts to a sentence. These parts are called the **complete subject** and the **complete predicate**.

The **complete subject** contains all the words that tell **who or what** the sentence is about.

The tiny white kitten snuggled beside its mother.

The subject and verb in a sentence should match with each other in number. A singular subject will have a singular verb, and a plural subject will have a plural verb.

In the sentence, underline all the words in the **complete subject**.

1. The shiny ladybug crawled on the leaf.

2. Several outgoing students performed in the school play.

3. The waves of the ocean crashed against the shore.

4. Many smart scientists conducted an experiment.

5. The playful otter slid down the riverbank.

6. My older brother Dylan moved across the country.

7. A lot of kids in my neighbourhood have pets.

Complete Predicates

The **complete predicate** includes the **verb** and all the words that tell about **what happened** in the sentence.

The forest fire crept closer to the town.

Every word in a sentence will be part the complete subject **or** part of the complete predicate.

Below, the complete subject is in bold, and the complete predicate is underlined.

***The happy puppies** chased a ball in our backyard.*

In the sentence, underline all the words in the **complete predicate**.

1. Five juicy oranges hung from the branches of the tree.

2. Many colourful balloons floated in the air at the birthday party.

3. The friendly mailman delivered letters to every house on the street.

4. The playful kittens chased each other around the living room.

5. Several red tractors plowed the farmer's fields.

6. The noisy construction trucks worked hard to build a new road.

7. The giggling children played a game of tag in the park.

What Comes at the End of a Sentence?

Put a **period** at the end of a **telling** *sentence*.

We are going to the park.

Put a **question mark** at the end of an **asking sentence**.

Did you bring your umbrella?

Put an **exclamation mark** at the end of a sentence that shows a **strong feeling**. Anger, happiness, and excitement are examples of strong feelings.

You hurt me! *This is fun!* *I can't wait!*

Put a **period** or an **exclamation mark** at the end of a **command** sentence.

A **command** sentence tells someone to do something.

Hang your coat up. *Watch out!*

1. Write a **telling** sentence.

____

2. Write an **asking** sentence.

____

3. Write a sentence that shows a **strong feeling**.

____

4. Write a **command** sentence.

____

What Comes at the End of a Sentence? (cont.)

5 Write the correct punctuation at the end of the sentence.

a) 

Did you finish your homework ☐

b) Wow, that's amazing ☐

c) 

Be careful with that vase ☐

d) Are you ready for the party ☐

e) 

Yay, we won the game ☐

f) Don't forget to brush your teeth ☐

g) 

Where did you put my toy ☐

One Sentence or Two?

A short sentence usually tells **one idea**.

Examples: My mother lost her ring. (one idea)

I found it in the bathroom. (one idea)

Be careful when you write sentences.

Check to see if you need to turn one sentence into two sentences.

*Example: This is **not** correct: I saw a puppy it was lost.*

*This is **correct**: I saw a puppy. It was lost.*

The sentence below is not correct.
Correct the sentence by writing it as two sentences.

1. The bird built a nest it was made of twigs.

____

2. It was windy I lost my hat.

____

3. Jack loves to swim he dives into the pool.

____

4. The teacher gave us homework it was hard.

____

5. The doorbell rang it was my friend Ali.

____

Joining Sentences with *And* or *But*

A **conjunction** is a word that joins together two short sentences.

The word **and** is a conjunction.

John bought crayons. He drew pictures.

John bought crayons, and he drew pictures.

The word **but** is used to join two contrasting ideas together.

Donna wants to stay up late. Her mom said no.

Donna wants to stay up late, but her mom said no.

1. Read the two sentences. Then use ***and*** or ***but*** to **join together** the two sentences. Write the **best word** to join the sentences.

a) Mia is good at math. She struggles with spelling.

Mia is good at math, ________ she struggles with spelling.

b) Timmy ran fast. He won the race.

Timmy ran fast, ________ he won the race.

2. The sentence below was made by joining together two short sentences. Complete the sentence by writing the joining word ***and*** or ***but***. Put a comma **before** the joining word.

a) The movie was scary ___________ I still enjoyed it.

b) Sarah likes to read books ____________ play soccer.

c) Ben went to the store __________ he forgot his wallet.

Joining Sentences with *Or* or *So*

Use ***or*** to join together two short sentences when each sentence tells about two **different** actions, and only **one** action will happen.

We can eat spaghetti for dinner tonight. We can eat chicken.

We can eat spaghetti for dinner tonight, or we can eat chicken.

Use ***so*** to join together two short sentences when the idea in the **second** sentence happens **because of** the idea in the **first** sentence.

It was raining. I took my umbrella.

It was raining, so I took my umbrella.

1 Write ***or*** or ***so*** to join together the sentences.

a) Is it sunny outside? Is it raining?

Is it sunny outside, _________ is it raining?

b) The store was closed. We couldn't buy any groceries.

The store was closed, _________ we couldn't buy any groceries.

2 The sentence below was made by joining together two short sentences. Write the joining word ***or*** or ***so***. Put a comma **before** the joining word.

a) Alexei might buy the blue bike _________ he might buy the red bike.

b) Polly loves to dance _________ she joined the ballet class.

c) I will either go to the park on Tuesday _________ on Thursday.

Sentences and Punctuation Review

1. In the sentence, underline all the words in the **complete subject**.

   a) The four cheesy pizzas smelled delicious.

   b) The tall funny clown entertained the children at the party.

2. In the sentence, underline all the words in the **complete predicate**.

   a) The water splashed everywhere when he jumped in the pool.

   b) The students finished their science homework before recess.

3. The sentence below is not correct. Correct each sentence by writing it as two sentences.

   a) He finished his homework he felt proud.

   ____

   b) The dog barked loudly it scared me.

   ____

4. Complete the sentence by writing the joining word ***and*** or ***but***.

   a) They went to the park __________ played on the swings.

   b) I was tired __________ I couldn't fall asleep.

5. Complete the sentence by writing the joining word ***or*** or ***so***.

   a) It's snowing outside __________ we need to wear warm clothes.

   b) I can choose to have an apple __________ an orange for a snack.

Unit 8

What Is a Contraction?

A **contraction** is one word made from two words, with one or more of the letters **left out**.

The letters that are left out are replaced by an **apostrophe** (').

Two Words	Contraction
I am	*I'm*
you are	*you're*
he is	*he's*
she is	*she's*

Two Words	Contraction
it is	*it's*
that is	*that's*
we are	*we're*
they are	*they're*

1 In the sentence, write the **contraction** for the words below the line.

a) I saw them at the park, and ________________ playing catch with a frisbee.
they are

b) ________________ so excited for my birthday party next week.
I am

c) ________________ going to be late for the meeting.
we are

d) Please be careful when ________________ crossing the street.
you are

2 Rewrite the sentence. Use **contractions** for the underlined words.

a) <u>She is</u> so happy that <u>it is</u> summer vacation next week.

____

b) <u>I am</u> feeling tired, but <u>that is</u> not going to stop me!

____

More Contractions

A **contraction** is one word made from two words, with one or more of the letters **left out**. The letters that are left out are replaced by an **apostrophe** ('). Below are examples of contractions made with the word ***will***.

Two Words	Contraction
I will	*I'll*
you will	*you'll*
he will	*he'll*

Two Words	Contraction
she will	*she'll*
we will	*we'll*
they will	*they'll*

1. In the sentence, write the **contraction** for the words below the line.

   a) ________________ have to wake up early tomorrow for our flight.
   (we will)

   b) If you follow the recipe carefully, ________________ bake a delicious cake.
   (you will)

   c) If he studies hard, ________________ pass the test.
   (he will)

   d) If you lend me your pen, ________________ give it back after the class.
   (I will)

2. Rewrite the sentences below. Write each **contraction** as two words.

   a) I'll help you with math and you'll help me with science. We'll both do great!

   ____

   ____

   ____

Abbreviations

An **abbreviation** is the **short form** of a word. An abbreviation ends with a **period**. The abbreviations in the sentence below are in bold.

*Example: **Mrs.** Lopez drove **Mr.** Rogers to the store.*

Mrs. is the abbreviation of ***mistress***, and ***Mr.*** is the abbreviation of ***mister***.

1 Circle the **correct choice** in brackets.

a) When I feel sick, my mom takes me to see (doctor Dr.) Mason.

b) We followed the (road Rd.) signs to the amusement park.

c) I rode my bike down Oak (street St.) to get to school this morning.

d) We walked down the (avenue Ave.), exploring the different shops.

e) We have art class with (mister Mr.) Bardot every Tuesday afternoon.

f) My (doctor Dr.) is located down Sarnia (road Rd.) on the corner.

2 Rewrite the sentence below to show the proper use of **abbreviations**.

a) Doctor Watson is best friends with mister Harris.

____

b) River ave. is near Storybook Street.

____

Contractions and Abbreviations Review

1 Rewrite the sentence. Use **contractions** for the underlined words.

a) I will wait for you, but we are leaving soon.

____

b) You are moving to a new city, and that is why I am sad.

____

2 Rewrite the sentence below. Write each **contraction** as two words.

We'll have to hurry if we're going to catch the bus before it's too late!

____

____

____

3 Circle the **correct choice** in brackets.

a) We visited the museum with (Dr. doctor) Parker, the archaeologist.

b) She bought a new book from (mister Mr.) Johnson's bookstore.

c) My house is the very last one on the (street St.).

d) The bakery on Maple (avenue Ave.) sells delicious pastries and cakes.

e) Drive down the (road Rd.) until you get to Jedmoore (road Rd.).

Unit 9

Homophones

Homophones are words that sound the same but are spelled differently and mean different things. *Example: right - write*

Fill in the blanks with the correct homophone from the word bank below.

blew	blue	meat	meet	right	their
there	too	two	weak	week	write

1. The sky is ______________ today.

   I ______________ bubbles with the wand.

2. Let's ______________ at the park after school.

   Mom cooked ______________ for dinner.

3. Please ______________ your name on the paper.

   Turn ______________ at the next corner.

4. They left ______________ jackets at home.

   The store is over ______________.

5. I have ______________ pencils in my bag.

   It's ______________ hot to go outside.

6. After the long ______________, I needed a break.

   The toy felt ______________ and it easily broke.

Homophones: There, Their, and They're

There refers to a place.

Their means belonging to them.

They're means *they are*.

Complete the sentence using ***there***, ***their***, or ***they're***.

1. I can see my house up ________________ on the hill.
2. The farmers harvested ________________ crops.
3. The students are excited because ________________ going on a field trip.
4. Arthur and Yamir picked up ________________ backpacks.
5. Can you reach the cookies up ________________ on the top shelf?
6. It's raining outside, so ________________ staying indoors to play.
7. The library is over ________________, next to the post office.
8. ________________ all painting pictures together.
9. The children put on ________________ helmets to go on a bike ride.

Synonyms and Antonyms

A **synonym** is a word that means the same as another word.
Example: cold - chilly

Circle the **synonym** for the bolded word in the sentence.

1. The rabbit **leaps** across the field. a) runs b) jumps

2. Sarah's face is filled with **joy**. a) anger b) happiness

3. Please **split** the cake into equal portions. a) divide b) connect

4. We share a moment of pure **happiness**. a) anger b) joy

5. The river **divides** the city into two parts. a) splits b) connects

An **antonym** is a word that means the opposite of another word.
Example: all - none

6. Draw a line to match the word with the related **antonym**.

loud	dark
happy	slow
fast	quiet
big	sad
light	small

Synonym, Antonym, and Homophone Review

ate	buy	bye	eight	their	there

1. Fill in the blank with the correct **homophone** from the word bank above.

   a) Yesterday, I ________________ a delicious sandwich for lunch.

   My little brother turns ________________ years old tomorrow.

   b) Is that your house over ________________?

   The students saw the teacher hang ________________ drawings on the wall.

   c) As the bell rang, we waved ________________ to our friends.

   I used my allowance to ________________ a toy from the store.

2. Write a **synonym** for the underlined word.

   a) The basement in our new house is <u>dirty.</u> ____________________

   b) I wore a jacket because it was <u>cold</u> outside. ____________________

   c) We found a <u>large</u> pumpkin at the farm. ____________________

3. Write an **antonym** for the underlined word.

   a) The science test was very <u>easy</u>. ____________________

   b) Our school's soccer team <u>won</u> the game. ____________________

   c) The road ahead is long and <u>straight.</u> ____________________

Unit 10

Context Clues

Read the sentence. Circle the answer that has the same meaning as the underlined word in the sentence. Use context clues to help.

1 The sun shining through the window was so brilliant it made my eyes hurt.

a) dull b) bright c) warm

2 Cathy walked slowly in an elegant white dress on her wedding day.

a) pretty b) ugly c) graceful

3 During Ed's hot shower, a lot of moisture collected on the mirror and walls.

a) water vapour b) dirt c) bugs

4 Moving the heavy potted plant into the dining room was quite an ordeal.

a) unhappy time b) dirty job c) difficult experience

5 Mary and Hank performed an experiment to see how the plant would react.

a) played out b) carried out c) took out

6 Grandma tried hard to recall what school was like when she was a little girl.

a) forget b) enjoy c) remember

7 Keith bugs his sister when he imitates everything she says and does.

a) ignores b) copies c) translates

8 The mother cat had to defend her kittens against the mean stray dog.

a) show off b) teach c) protect

Context Clues (cont.)

Read the sentence. Circle the answer that has the same meaning as the underlined word in the sentence. Use context clues to help.

9. The old dog was very <u>frail</u> and had to be helped up the stairs.

a) strong b) weak c) sad

10. Sami lives on the <u>border</u> between Alberta and Saskatchewan.

a) edge b) street c) boundary line

11. Max says he needs to <u>chill</u> the dough in the fridge to make it firmer.

a) make it cold b) make it hot c) bake it

12. The new paper towels do not <u>absorb</u> liquids as well as the old brand did.

a) eat b) soak up c) create

13. Wayne's baby sister <u>grasped</u> his finger with her tiny hand and smiled at him.

a) grabbed and held b) understood c) pushed away

14. We ran from the car to the store during a short <u>pause</u> in the rain storm.

a) vacation b) drying up c) temporary stop

15. Ken used the globe in the classroom to <u>locate</u> Australia.

a) get addresses for b) see c) find the exact position of

16. Doctors were <u>mystified</u> about how the woman got better without medicine.

a) puzzled b) happy c) angry

Unit 1

We Need a Class Pet

Dear Mr. Cabos,

I think we should get a pet hamster for our class! It would be cool! Let me tell you why.

First, it would make our classroom exciting. We can watch the hamster run and have fun. We can take turns feeding it and giving it water. It can be a special class job!

Next, having a hamster as our class pet will teach us about taking care of animals. We can make a cozy and safe home for the hamster. We will clean the cage and give the hamster healthy food.

Another reason is that a hamster can help us feel relaxed and happy. School can be tough. Playing with the hamster during breaks can make us feel better. We can share the fun with friends, too!

We promise to take good care of the hamster. We will make a schedule and clean its cage together.

Having a pet hamster in our class would be amazing! I hope you will let us have one.

Sincerely,

Sara

We Need a Class Pet – Think About It!

Persuasive writing is when you try to convince someone to agree with your ideas or to do something you want them to do. You do this by giving good reasons and examples in your writing. It's like trying to win a friendly argument using your words!

1. What is the purpose of the letter?

    a) To persuade Mr. Cabos to get a pet hamster for the class

    b) To inform the class about the benefits of having a pet hamster

    c) To discuss different types of pets suitable for the classroom

    d) To share a personal story about a pet hamster

2. Who is the intended audience of the letter?

    a) Sara b) Mr. Cabos

    c) classmates d) hamster owners

3. Do you agree with Sara that a hamster would make a good classroom pet? Explain your thinking.

____

____

____

____

We Need a Class Pet – Think About It! (cont.)

4. Congratulations! Mr. Cabos has approved the request to have a pet hamster in the class. Using information from the reading and your own ideas, create a list of tasks for taking care of the hamster.

5. Design and label a perfect home or cage for the new pet hamster.

We Need a Class Pet – Think About It! (cont.)

6. Many kids in your class want to have longer recess time, but some teachers are not sure. Write a persuasive letter to your teacher, explaining why longer recess time is important.

____
DATE

Dear ______________________,
GREETING

BODY

____

____

____

____

____

____

____

____

____

Sincerely,

____
CLOSING / SIGNATURE

- ☐ I used capitals and end marks.
- ☐ I used linking words to connect my ideas.
- ☐ I organized my ideas in a way that makes sense.

Unit 2

Birds and Bats

Birds and bats are both animals that can fly. In some ways, these animals are the same. In other ways, these animals are very different.

Bird

Bat

Wings: A bird's wings are covered with feathers. A bat's wings have no feathers.

Food: Some kinds of bats eat fruit and seeds, and so do some kinds of birds. Many birds and bats eat insects. Some insects can eat up the plants that farmers grow. Birds and bats help farmers by eating some of these insects.

Sleeping: Bats sleep hanging upside down. Some birds sleep standing up, and other sit down to sleep. Birds and bats sleep at different times. Most birds sleep at night, but most bats sleep during the day. Animals that sleep during the day and are active at night are called nocturnal animals.

Bats sleeping

Babies: Baby bats do not hatch from eggs, but baby birds do. Baby bats drink milk from their mothers. Baby birds are fed by their parents. The parents might catch worms and insects to feed to their babies.

Homes: Many birds build nests. Most birds build nests in trees, but some birds build nests on the ground. Bats do not build nests. They often use caves, trees, or barns as homes.

Bird nest

Bats in a cave

Fact Box — Are Vampire Bats Real?

Yes, there really are vampire bats that drink blood! They bite sleeping animals to make a little blood come out. The animals do not die after losing only a little blood. Vampire bats almost never bite humans.

Birds and Bats – Think About It!

Compare and contrast text is a type of writing that tells you how two things are alike (compare) and how they are different (contrast).

1. Why did the author write this text about birds and bats?

    a) To make the readers happy and interested in learning about them

    b) To convince readers to protect and take care of bird and bat homes

    c) To teach and show us how birds and bats are alike and different

    d) To tell a story about the author's own adventure with birds and bats

2. Fill in the Venn diagram to compare and contrast birds and bats.

- active at night
- lay eggs
- babies drink milk
- have wings
- sleep upside down
- have feathers
- help farmers

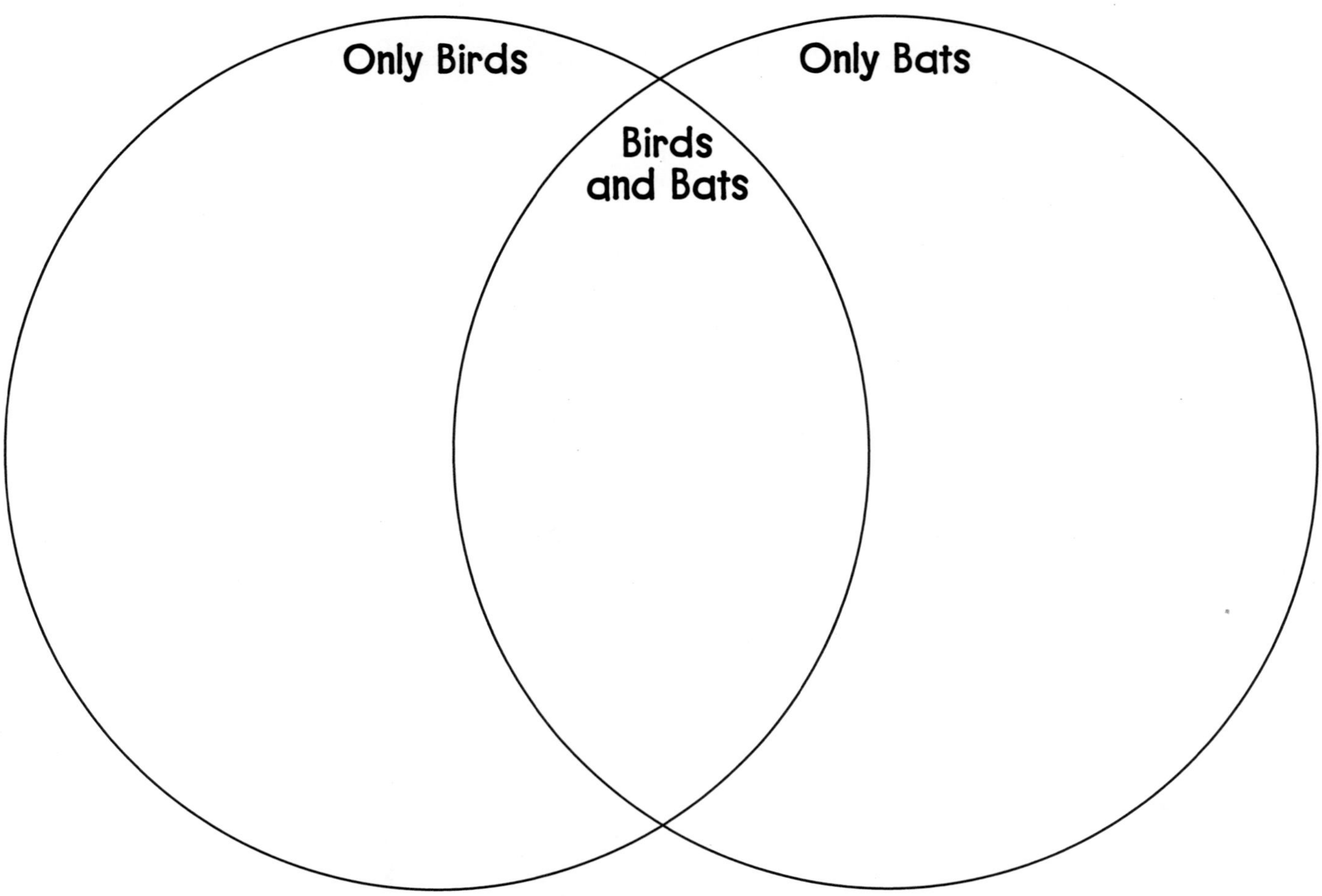

Birds and Bats – Think About It! (cont.)

A **heading** is the title given to a part of a text.

3. Circle the section heading where baby bats and baby birds are discussed.

a) Wings b) Food c) Sleeping d) Babies e) Homes

4. Define the term "nocturnal animals."

____

5. Using information from the reading and your own ideas, fill in the chart.

✓ **Fact** A statement that can be proven to be true.
Opinion A feeling or belief about something.

Birds and Bats – Think About It! (cont.)

6 Complete the crossword puzzle.

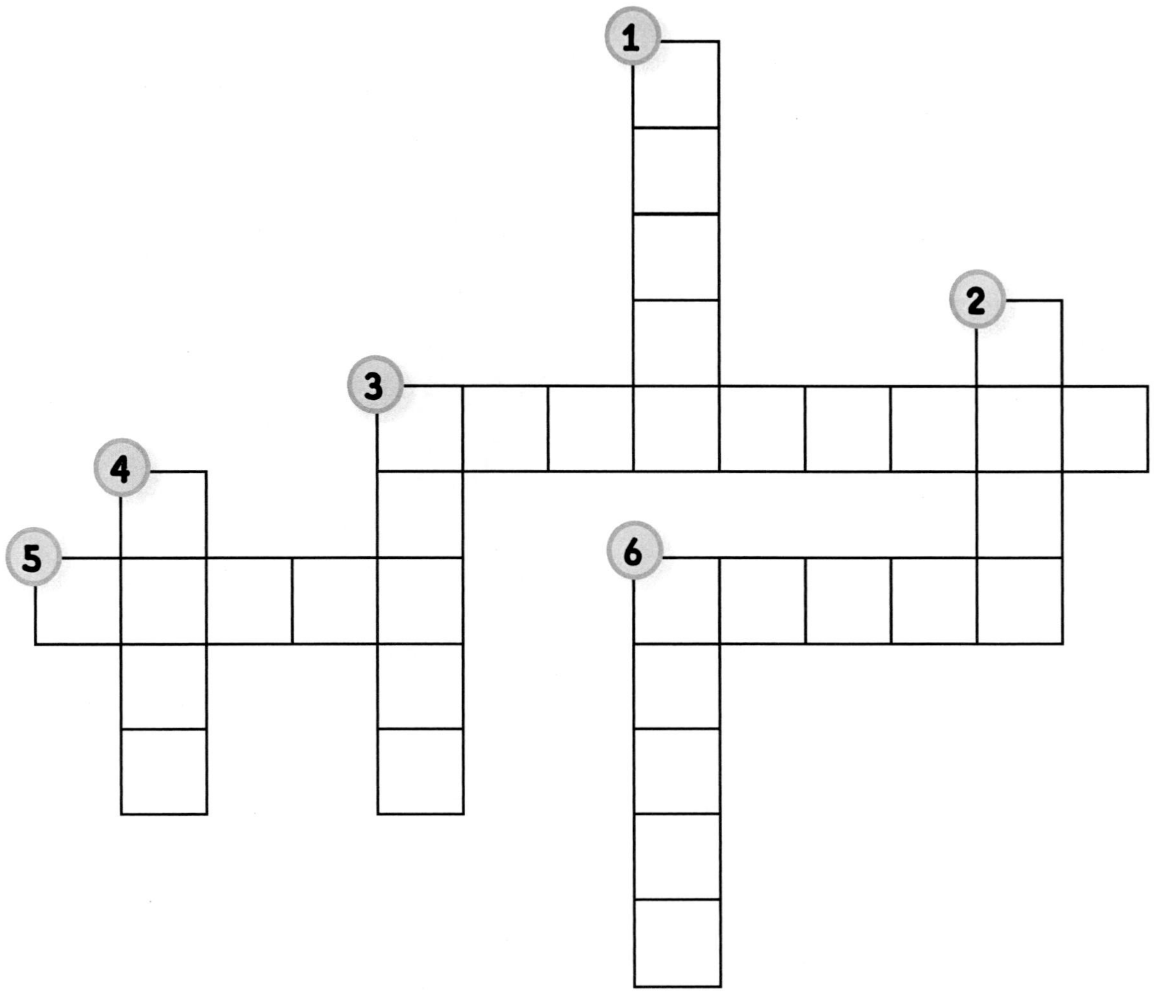

Across

3. A word for animals that sleep during the day and are active at night

5. Body parts used for flying

6. A type of animal that has feathers and can fly

Down

1. Some kinds of bats eat this

2. Animals that sleep hanging upside down

3. Birds build these

4. Baby bats drink this from their mothers

6. Vampire bats drink this

Unit 3

Mouse and Lion

Lion was taking a nap in the forest. He opened his eyes when he felt tiny feet running across his nose. A mouse! Lion put out one of his huge paws and trapped Mouse under it. "You woke me up!" roared grumpy Lion. "Now I will eat you."

Mouse wiggled, but she could not get free. "Please let me go!" she cried. "If you let me go, I promise that someday I will do something to help you."

Lion laughed. How could a tiny mouse ever help a big lion? But Lion had a kind heart, so he let Mouse go anyway.

A few days later, Lion was walking in the forest. He was busy looking for his next meal, so he did not watch where he was going. He did not see that he was about to step right into a trap a hunter had set!

Suddenly, Lion found himself trapped in a net made of thick rope. He tried and tried, but he could not escape from the net. He was so angry that he let out two loud roars.

Mouse heard Lion's roars. "It sounds like Lion is in trouble!" she said. "I must find him to see if I can help." Mouse ran through the forest until she found Lion.

"Don't worry," Mouse said to Lion. "My teeth are small, but they are sharp and good at chewing." Mouse chewed through the ropes in the net until Lion was able to escape from the trap.

"Thank you, little friend," said Lion. "Now I know that a tiny mouse really can help a big lion."

Mouse and Lion – Think About It!

A **fable** is a short story that teaches a lesson. It has animals that talk and act like humans. The animals in the fable help us learn about life and how to behave.

1 What lesson can we learn from this fable?

a) Big animals are always stronger than small animals.

b) It's important to be kind to others, no matter their size.

c) Lions and mice can never be friends.

d) Forest traps are dangerous for all animals.

2 Which title below would also work well for this story?

a) Lion Makes a Promise
b) Mouse Gets Lost
c) Mouse Keeps Her Promise
d) Lion's Sharp Teeth

3 Who woke Lion up from his nap?

a) A hunter
b) Another lion
c) A mouse
d) A rabbit

4 Why did Lion want to eat the mouse at first?

a) Because the mouse woke the lion up

b) Because the mouse promised to help him someday

c) Because the mouse was trapped under Lion's paw

d) Because Lion was hungry

Mouse and Lion – Think About It! (cont.)

5. What did Mouse promise to do for Lion?

   a) Catch his next meal
   b) Find him a new home
   c) Do something to help him
   d) Sing him a lullaby

6. How did Mouse help Lion when he was trapped in a net?

   a) Mouse called for help from other animals.
   b) Mouse chewed through the ropes in the net.
   c) Mouse distracted the hunter while Lion escaped.

7. In the text, Mouse says, "Please let me go! If you let me go, I promise that someday I will do something to help you." Why do you think Mouse made this promise to Lion?

   ____

   ____

8. "My teeth are small, but they are sharp and good at chewing." What does Mouse mean by saying her teeth are sharp and good at chewing?

   ____

9. "Now I know that a tiny mouse really can help a big lion." What did Lion learn from Mouse's help?

   ____

Mouse and Lion – Think About It! (cont.)

10. Imagine you are Mouse from the story. Write a diary entry describing your encounter with Lion and how you felt when you promised to help him.

Draw a picture.

- ☐ I used capitals and end marks.
- ☐ I used linking words to connect my ideas.
- ☐ I organized my ideas in a way that makes sense.

Unit 4 The World's Tallest Animal

Giraffes are amazing creatures that hold the title of being the tallest animals in the world. Let's explore their incredible features and learn more about giraffes.

What Do They Look Like?

Giraffes have special features that make them one-of-a-kind. They have long legs and a long neck, which help them reach the leaves on tall trees. Their bodies are covered in beautiful brown spots, but you won't find any spots on the bottom part of their legs. Giraffes also have a very long tongue that can be black, blue, or purple. This remarkable tongue allows them to easily grab leaves and pull them off trees.

Where Do They Live?

Giraffes live in Africa, where there are plenty of trees. They prefer areas with lots of vegetation because that's where they find their favourite food—leaves!

Life as a Baby Giraffe

Even as babies, giraffes are quite tall! When a baby giraffe is born, it is already as tall as an adult human. Amazing, right? And guess what? Baby giraffes can walk just one hour after they are born. It's so different from human babies, who take much longer to start walking.

Giraffes are truly remarkable animals. Their tall height, long necks, and unique spots make them stand out in the animal kingdom. So next time you see a picture of a giraffe or visit a zoo, remember how unique and interesting these gentle giants are!

The World's Tallest Animal – Think About It!

An **informational text** helps us learn about a topic by giving us facts and details.

1 What is the author's purpose in writing this text?

a) To inform readers about giraffes and their unique features

b) To entertain readers with a funny story about giraffes

c) To persuade readers to buy giraffe-themed merchandise

d) To share personal opinions about giraffes

2 According to the text, where do giraffes live?

a) North America　　b) Africa　　c) Europe

3 How tall is a baby giraffe when it is born?

a) As tall as a baby elephant

b) As tall as a dog

c) As tall as an adult human

4 According to the text, what does the vocabulary word "vegetation" refer to?

a) Tall trees in the giraffe's habitat

b) The spots on a giraffe's body

c) The favourite food of giraffes—leaves

d) The long legs of a giraffe

The World's Tallest Animal – Think About It! (cont.)

A **main idea** is what the text is mostly about.

A **heading** is the title given to a part of a text.

A **detail** is important information that tells more about the main idea.

5 Fill in the boxes using information from the text.

Main idea

Heading	Heading	Heading
Details	Details	Details

The World's Tallest Animal – Think About It! (cont.)

6 Think about what makes giraffes special, like their long necks, spots, and being tall. Along the outline of the giraffe shape, write words or short phrases that describe giraffes. Colour the giraffe and add a background.

Unit 5

My Super Racecar

The Super Racecar is a sleek, shiny, fast toy. It's made of bright red plastic and has cool black stripes from the front to the back. The wheels are silver and polished. They spin smoothly as the car zooms across the floor. When I hold the car, it feels smooth and not too heavy.

The car has big, round headlights that shine bright. It also has a small grille that looks like a smile. On the trunk, a special part called a spoiler helps the car stay steady during fast races. When I press a button on the roof, the car makes engine sounds just like a real racecar!

The Super Racecar is the fastest toy car I have. When I pull it back and let it go, it speeds forward quickly, leaving a trail of excitement behind. It's fun to race it with my friends and see whose car is the fastest.

To sum it up, the Super Racecar is an awesome toy. We learned about its bright colours, smooth body, shiny wheels, and fast speed. Describing things helps us imagine and understand them better by using specific details.

Now, it's your turn to describe your favourite toy or object using your words!

My Super Racecar – Think About It!

Descriptive writing uses words to create a picture in your mind. It helps us imagine how things look, feel, sound, and even smell!

1. What does a descriptive text help us do?

    a) Solve problems

    b) Imagine and understand things better

    c) Persuade others

    d) Create stories

2. Think about what the word *describe* means. Put a check mark in the box beside each sentence that describes something.

    a) ☐ The clouds in the sky are white and fluffy.

    b) ☐ Is it your birthday today?

    c) ☐ The ice is cold and slippery.

3. Draw a line to match the word with its meaning.

Shiny	Moves smoothly and quickly
Spoiler	Helps the car stay steady during races
Imagine	Reflects light and looks glossy
Fast	Picture or visualize something in your mind

My Super Racecar – Think About It! (cont.)

4. Read the statement carefully. Determine whether the statement is true or false. Circle your answer.

a) T F Descriptive writing helps us imagine and understand things better.

b) T F The Super Racecar is made of green plastic.

c) T F The wheels of the car are black and dull.

d) T F The spoiler on top of the car makes engine sounds.

e) T F Pulling back the Super Racecar makes it go faster.

5. Write each adjective from the text in the correct category in the chart below. Remember to place each adjective in only one category.

big	bright	cool	fast	round
shiny	silver	sleek	smooth	

Category 1: Appearance	Category 2: Texture	Category 3: Speed

My Super Racecar – Think About It! (cont.)

6. Design your own racecar and describe it using descriptive writing. Include details about its appearance, features, and what makes it special.

☐ I used capitals and end marks. ☐ I used linking words to connect my ideas.

☐ I organized my ideas in a way that makes sense. ☐ I included descriptive words.

Unit 6

My Morning Routine

Every morning, I do things in a specific order to prepare for the day. First, I wake up and stretch my arms and legs. Then, I go to the bathroom to wash my face. After that, I put on my clothes, tie my shoes, and brush my hair.

Next, I head to the kitchen for breakfast. I pour cereal into a bowl, add milk, and eat it with a spoon. Sometimes, I have toast with jam, too. Once I finish eating, I wash my dishes and clean the table. Then I brush my teeth.

After breakfast, it's time to get my school bag ready. First, I put my books and notebooks inside it. Next, I check for everything I need. Then, I grab my backpack and head out the door.

To sum it up, the sequence text helps us understand the order in which events happen. For example, I follow a specific sequence of actions in my morning routine to prepare for the day. The article tells us about each step one by one to show how the sequence works. Now, think about your morning routine and the order of what you do.

My Morning Routine – Think About It!

A **sequence text** is like following a step-by-step guide. It helps us understand the order of events and how things happen.

1. What is a sequence?

   a) A step-by-step guide   b) Something you wear on your feet

2. Number the sentences in the correct order to show the sequence of events.

   ______ I wake up and stretch my arms and legs.

   ______ I head to the kitchen for breakfast.

   ______ I go to the bathroom to wash my face.

   ______ I check for everything I need in my school bag.

   ______ I put on my clothes, tie my shoes, and brush my hair.

   ______ I grab my backpack and head out the door.

   ______ I wash my dishes, clean the table, then brush my teeth.

3. List three compound words found in the text.

____

A **caption** tells what a picture is about.

4. Write a caption for the picture in the text.

My Morning Routine – Think About It! (cont.)

5. Which of the following best describes the purpose of a sequence text?

   a) To entertain the reader with a story

   b) To persuade the reader to take action

   c) To describe how something looks or feels

   d) To explain the order of events and how things happen

6. Unscramble the words to form a sentence that is related to the morning routine described in the text.

   a) kitchen head to next breakfast the for I.

   ____

   b) sometimes I jam, too have with toast.

   ____

   c) inside my put I books and notebooks first it.

   ____

   d) and up stretch I and arms my legs wake.

   ____

My Morning Routine – Think About It! (cont.)

7. Write a step-by-step description of your own morning routine. Include at least five actions or tasks that you do in a specific order to get ready.

Draw a picture.

☐ I used capitals and end marks. ☐ I used linking words to connect my ideas.

☐ I organized my ideas in a way that makes sense.

Unit 7

Dad's Birthday

Mom took me into my bedroom to tell me a secret. "Liam, your dad's birthday is on Sunday. This year, we're going to have a surprise party for him," she whispered. "We'll have the party on Saturday to make sure he's surprised. I've invited lots of people to come."

I was excited about the surprise party! Last year on Dad's birthday, we had a small party with just Dad, Mom, Grandma, Grandpa, and me. It wasn't a surprise party, but it was fun. A big surprise party would be even more fun!

Mom showed me the present she got for Dad. It was a red wool sweater. Last year, he got a red sweater for his birthday and he loved it. But then it got put in the dryer by mistake. The sweater shrank and was too small for him to wear.

Suddenly, I realized I didn't have a present for Dad. Last year, I made him a card, but I wanted do something special for his surprise party. That's when I had a great idea. Instead of a card, I would make him a little birthday book!

I stapled together five sheets of paper. On the cover, I wrote "Happy SURPRISE Birthday!" in big letters. On each of the other pages, I drew a picture of something Dad and I had done together in the past year. I drew the time we went fishing, the time we soaked each other with the hose, the time we went to a baseball game, and the time we made a snowman. I wrote a caption for each picture to tell what it was about.

The party was fun, and Dad was very surprised. I gave him his birthday book after he had opened his other presents. He was very quiet as he read it, and he spent time looking at each picture. When he got to the end, he wiped a tear from his eye. I was crushed! Dad didn't like my present! Then he hugged me and said, "Thank you, Liam. I like your gift best of all. Sometimes grownups get a tear or two when they are very happy. Your birthday book makes me very, very happy!"

Dad's Birthday – Think About It!

Narrative text is a type of writing used to tell a story. It can be a real story about something that happened to you, like your first day at school, or it can be a made-up story about anything you can imagine, like a space adventure with alien friends!

1. What kind of narrative text is this?

   a) a real story   b) a made up story

2. Liam says, "I was crushed!" What does this mean?

   a) I was very excited.
   b) I was feeling sick.
   c) I was very disappointed.
   d) I was not surprised.

3. Complete the sentence to tell how many pictures Liam drew in the birthday book.

   Liam drew ________________ pictures in Dad's birthday book.

A **cause** is what makes something happen.
The **effect** is what happens because of the cause.

4. Write **cause** or **effect** beside the sentence.

a) ________________: Dad's red sweater got put in the dryer.

b) ________________: The sweater shrank and was too small for him.

Dad's Birthday – Think About It! (cont.)

5 The text tells about Dad's birthday parties this year and last year. Write each piece of information in the correct box.

- Liam made something for Dad
- is not on his birthday
- is a big party
- Dad gets a red sweater

Both of Dad's Birthday Parties	Only Dad's Surprise Party

6 Draw a line to match the person with what they said in the story.

Liam's Mom

"Sometimes grownups get a tear or two when they are very happy."

Liam's Dad

"We'll have the party on Saturday to make sure he's surprised."

7 What do you think would be the ultimate way to spend your birthday?

Dad's Birthday – Think About It! (cont.)

8 Have you ever had a surprise party for someone in your family or for a friend? How did you feel about keeping the party a secret? Share your experience.

Draw a picture.

☐ I used capitals and end marks. ☐ I used linking words to connect my ideas.

☐ I organized my ideas in a way that makes sense.

Wolves and Dogs

A wolf looks like a big dog, but wolves and dogs are different animals. Wolves and dogs are the same in some ways, but they are different in other ways.

Grey wolf

What They Look Like

Adult dogs can be different sizes — small, medium-size, or large. All adult wolves are about the same size.

Adult dogs and adult wolves both have 42 teeth. Wolves have larger and stronger teeth than dogs.

German Shepherd Dog

Most dogs have brown eyes, but a few dogs have blue eyes. All wolves have eyes that are a golden-brown colour called amber.

Things They Do

Both dogs and wolves use their voices to make sounds. Dogs usually bark when they make sounds. A bark is a short sound like *woof*. Wolves usually howl. A howl is a long sound like *ah-ooooo*.

Wolf howling

Wolves are shy animals. They do not like to be around people. If they see people coming, they will usually run away. Dogs love to be around people. They can get lonely when there are no people around.

Dogs and wolves have more than one baby at a time. A group of babies born at the same time is called a litter. Young dogs and wolves are called pups or puppies.

Golden Retriever

Wolves and Dogs – Think About It!

Compare and contrast text is a type of writing that tells you how two things are alike (compare) and how they are different (contrast).

1. Fill in the Venn diagram to compare and contrast wolves and dogs.

- all have the same eye colour
- have more than one baby at a time
- like to be around people
- do not like to be near people
- adults have 42 teeth
- usually bark

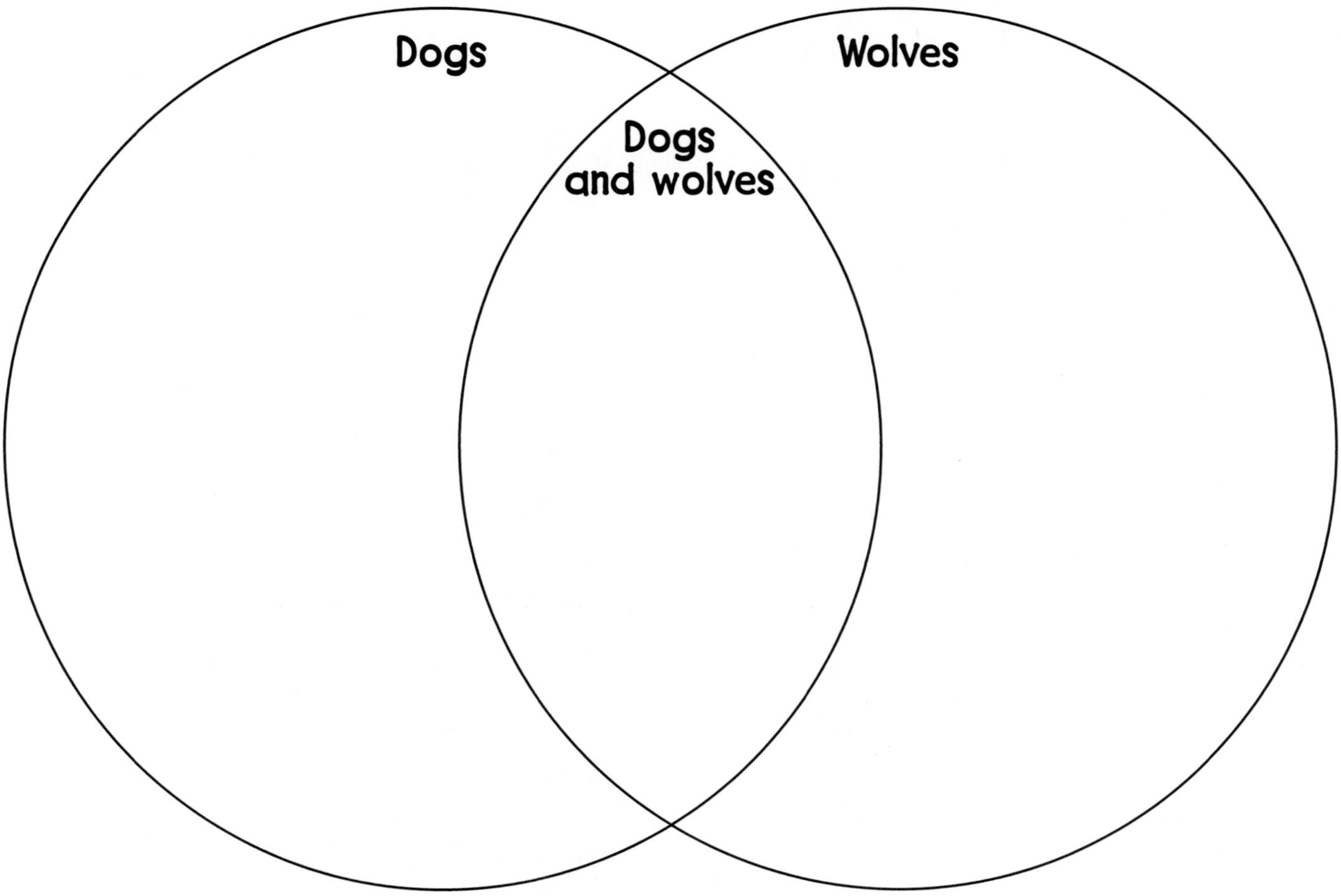

2. Wolves do not like to be around people. What does this tell you about wolves?

a) Wolves like to live near cities.
b) Wolves make good pets.
c) Wolves do not make good pets.
d) Wolves are good hunters.

Wolves and Dogs – Think About It! (cont.)

3 Complete the crossword puzzle.

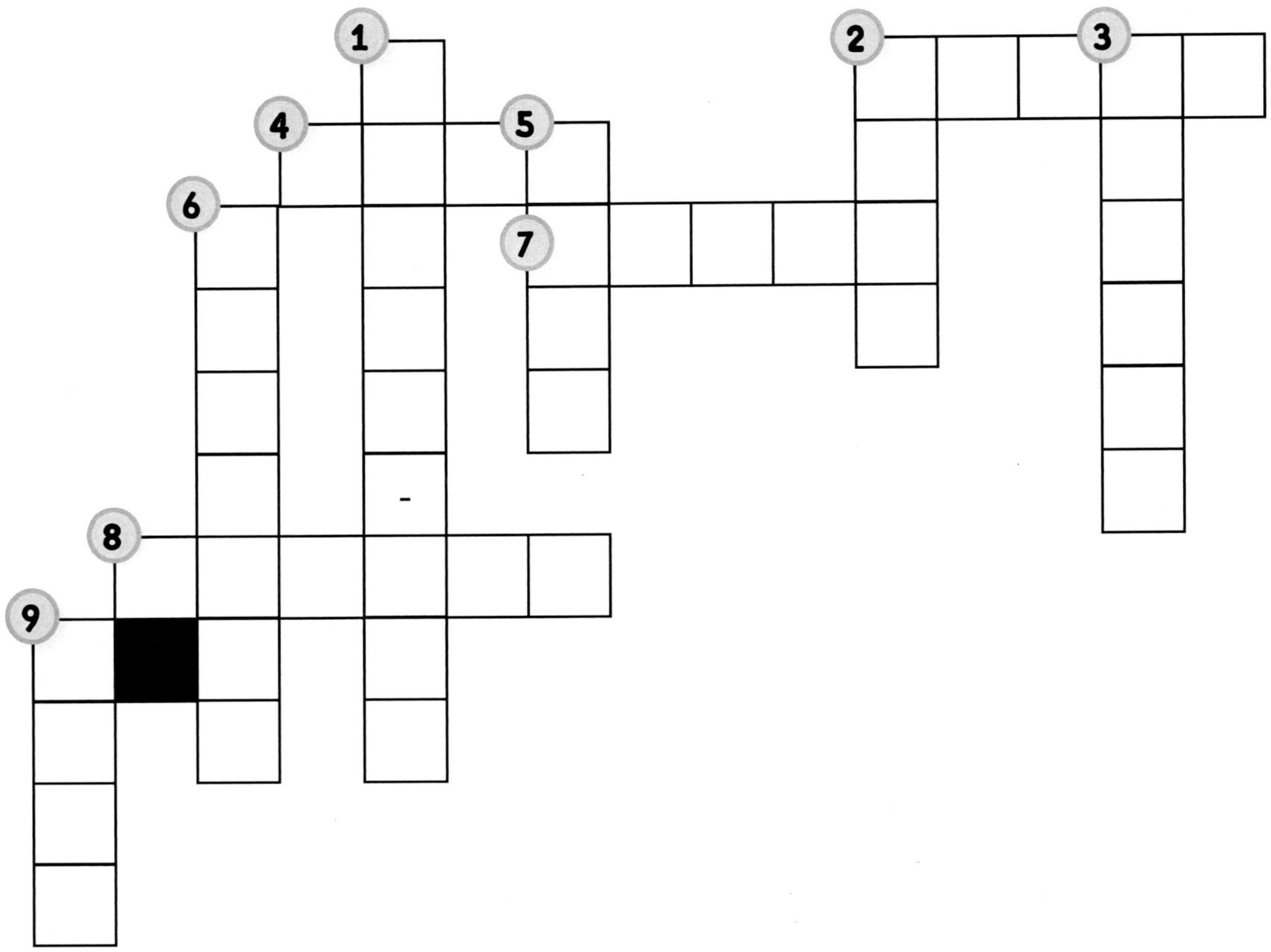

Across

2. Colour of eyes in most dogs

4. Animals that love to be around people

7. Colour of eyes in wolves

8. Group of babies born at the same time

Down

1. Wolves and dogs have this number of teeth

2. The sound made by dogs

3. Animals that don't like to be around people

5. The sizes of all adult wolves

6. Young wolves and dogs are called this

9. The sound wolves usually make

Wolves and Dogs – Think About It! (cont.)

4. What is your favourite animal? How does it compare to wolves or dogs? Explain.

Draw a picture.

☐ I used capitals and end marks. ☐ I used linking words to connect my ideas.

☐ I organized my ideas in a way that makes sense. ☐ I included comparisons.

Viola Desmond

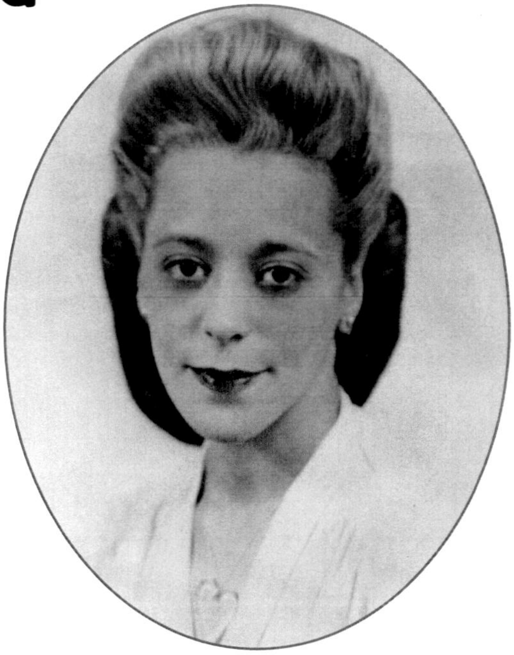

Viola Desmond was an amazing Black businesswoman. She was born in Halifax, Nova Scotia, in 1914 and she made a big impact. Viola strongly believed in treating everyone fairly and with kindness. She owned a beauty shop where she helped people feel beautiful inside and out. With her strong will, Viola became an inspiration to many people.

Unfair Movie Theatre

One day, Viola Desmond went to watch a movie at a theatre in her hometown, Halifax. The theatre workers told Viola she had to sit in a different area—the balcony. They told her this only because of the colour of her skin. This upset Viola because she knew it wasn't fair. So, she decided not to go to the balcony, but to take seat in the main part of the theatre. Because she didn't follow their unfair rule, the theatre staff called the police, and she was taken to jail. This was a hard experience for Viola, but her bravery inspired other people to stand up for fairness, too.

Viola Desmond on the Ten-Dollar Bill

Did you know Viola Desmond's picture is on Canada's ten-dollar bill? It's to remember her for fighting for something important called *equality*. Equality means treating everyone the same, no matter what they look like or where they come from.

Making a Difference

Viola's story teaches us that we can all make a difference. She said, "I want the right to sit anywhere I choose." Her bravery made her a hero from Nova Scotia. Her story reminds us to be kind and fair to everyone. We can all help make the world better, just like Viola did.

Viola Desmond – Think About It!

A **biography** is a text that tells true and interesting facts about a person's life.

1 What tells us that this text is a biography?

a) The text is all about a pretend character's journey

b) The text tells us how to do something step-by-step

c) The text is about a real person, Viola Desmond, and her life

2 With her strong will, Viola became an inspiration to many people. "Inspiration" means:

a) someone who encourages and motivates others

b) feeling tired and lazy

c) a feeling of happiness

A **heading** is the title given to a part of a text.

3 Under which heading can we learn about what Viola's story teaches us?

a) Unfair Movie Theatre

b) Viola Desmond on the Ten-Dollar Bill

c) Making a Difference

4 What problem did Viola face at the movie theatre and how did she respond?

a) The movie was sold out, so she bought a ticket for a different show.

b) She was told to sit in the balcony because of her skin colour, but she refused to go there.

c) She couldn't find her seat, so she asked a theatre worker for help.

Viola Desmond – Think About It! (cont.)

5. What does *equality* mean according to the text?

   a) Only treating friends the same

   b) Treating everyone the same, no matter what they look like

   c) Only treating family members the same

6. Why do you think it is important to treat everyone the same, no matter what they look like or where they come from?

   ____

   ____

7. Read the statement carefully. Determine whether the statement is true or false. Circle your answer.

   a) T F Viola Desmond was born in Halifax, Nova Scotia.

   b) T F Viola Desmond owned a bakery shop.

   c) T F Viola Desmond was asked to sit in the balcony area of the movie theatre.

   d) T F Viola Desmond followed the unfair rule and moved to the balcony.

   e) T F Viola Desmond's picture is on Canada's twenty-dollar bill.

Viola Desmond – Think About It! (cont.)

8 Think of someone you would choose to be on the ten-dollar bill. Design a new bill for this person. Explain your thinking.

☐ I used capitals and end marks.
☐ I used linking words to connect my ideas.
☐ I organized my ideas in a way that makes sense.

Making Cheese

Some cheeses are soft, like ricotta, while others are hard, like cheddar. There are runny cheeses, too, like Brie. Learn how to make your own cheese from scratch.

Materials:

- fresh milk (from a cow, goat, or sheep)
- salt
- stove and refrigerator
- cutting utensils
- cultures and rennet (bacteria)
- cream separator
- cheese cloth or strainer
- cans for milk storage

Procedure:

Making cheese

Step One: Milk Collection

1. Milk the animals and collect fresh milk in cans.
2. Check the milk to see if it has enough butter fat.

Step Two: Cream Separation

1. Pour the milk into a special machine called a cream separator.
2. Use the machine to separate the cream and make butter.

Step Three: Milk Ripening

1. Heat the rest of the milk and cultures and rennet to make it thick.

Step Four: Curd Formation

1. Cut the thickened milk into little cubes to make something called curds.

Step Five: Curd Treatment

1. Warm up the curds gently to make them even more solid.
2. Squeeze the liquid out of the curds.

Step Six: Salting and Curing

1. Sprinkle salt on the curds to make them taste even better.
2. Refrigerate the curds until they become the texture and taste you like.

Making Cheese – Think About It!

A **procedural text** is like a recipe or a set of instructions. It tells you the steps you need to follow to make something or do something.

1. What is the purpose of this text?

   a) To entertain b) To explain something step by step

2. Cheese is made from which main ingredient?

   a) Fresh milk b) Water c) Salt

3. What is the purpose of a cream separator?

   a) To ripen and thicken the milk b) To make butter separately

4. What is the name of the process of making curds?

   a) Cream separation b) Milk collection c) Curd formation

5. How do you make the curds more solid?

   a) Squeeze out the liquid b) Add more milk
   c) Heat the curds gently

6. Number the steps of the cheese-making process in the correct order.

   ______ Curd Formation ______ Cream Separation

   ______ Milk Ripening ______ Curd Treatment

   ______ Milk Collection ______ Salting and Curing

Making Cheese – Think About It! (cont.)

7. What is the final step in making cheese?

a) Milk collection b) Salting and curing c) Cream separation

8. Fill in the blanks with the correct words from the word bank.

butter	cream	cubes	cultures
curds	fresh	salt	

a) Cheese is made from ______________ milk.

b) The ____________ separator separates the cream from the milk.

c) ____________ and rennet are added to ripen and thicken the ____________.

d) The thickened milk is cut into _______________ to make curds.

e) _______________ is sprinkled on the curds to enhance flavor.

f) The cream separator is used to make _______________ separately.

9. Unscramble the words below to reveal different kinds of cheeses.

brie	gouda	feta	parmesan	ricotta	swiss

a) sisws __________________ b) repsaman __________________

c) erbi __________________ d) aodug __________________

e) atfe __________________ f) atotirc __________________

Making Cheese – Think About It! (cont.)

An **idiom** is a special saying that has a hidden meaning. It is not meant to be taken literally. Instead, it's a fun and creative way to express an idea or feeling.

10 Draw the idiom.

"The big cheese"

Literal Meaning what is exactly written	**Figurative Meaning** the creative meaning of the words

11 Explain what you think the idiom means.

____

____

12 If you were "the big cheese" of your school, what changes would you make?

____

____

____

☐ I used capitals and end marks. ☐ My printing is neat. ☐ My writing makes sense.

Unit 12

Spiders

Big and Small

There are different kinds of spiders. Most spiders are quite small. Some are so tiny that they are hard to see. The largest spider is as big as a dinner plate! You won't run into that kind of spider unless you go to a forest in South America.

Spider Webs

Spiders' bodies have spinnerets. These are like little spinning machines on their bodies. Spinnerets help spiders make thin threads called silk. The silk threads are very sticky. Spiders use them to build their webs.

Webs are how spiders catch insects to eat. When an insect flies into a web, it tries to get away but it can't. It's stuck! The insect will be the spider's lunch!

Spider Senses

Since most spiders can't see very well, they use their feelers to tell if an insect is in their web. The insect pulls the web as it tries to get away. The spider can feel the web moving, so it knows there is an insect caught in the web. But not all spiders build webs. Some have other ways of catching food.

Are Spiders Insects?

Many people think spiders are insects. Why? Most spiders and most insects are very small creatures, and spiders and insects both have more than two legs. But spiders are not insects. Insects have six legs, and spiders have eight legs. Also, insects have wings. There are no spiders that have wings.

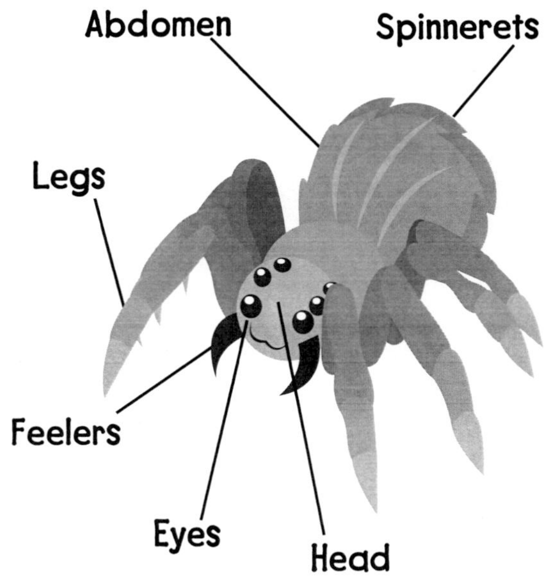

How Spiders Help Us

Spiders eat many insects people don't like, such as mosquitoes and fleas. Spiders also eat insects that can harm farmers' crops. Scientists are investigating ways to make new medicines from spiders.

Spiders – Think About It!

1 Fill in the diagram using information from the text.

abdomen	eyes	feelers	head	legs	spinnerets

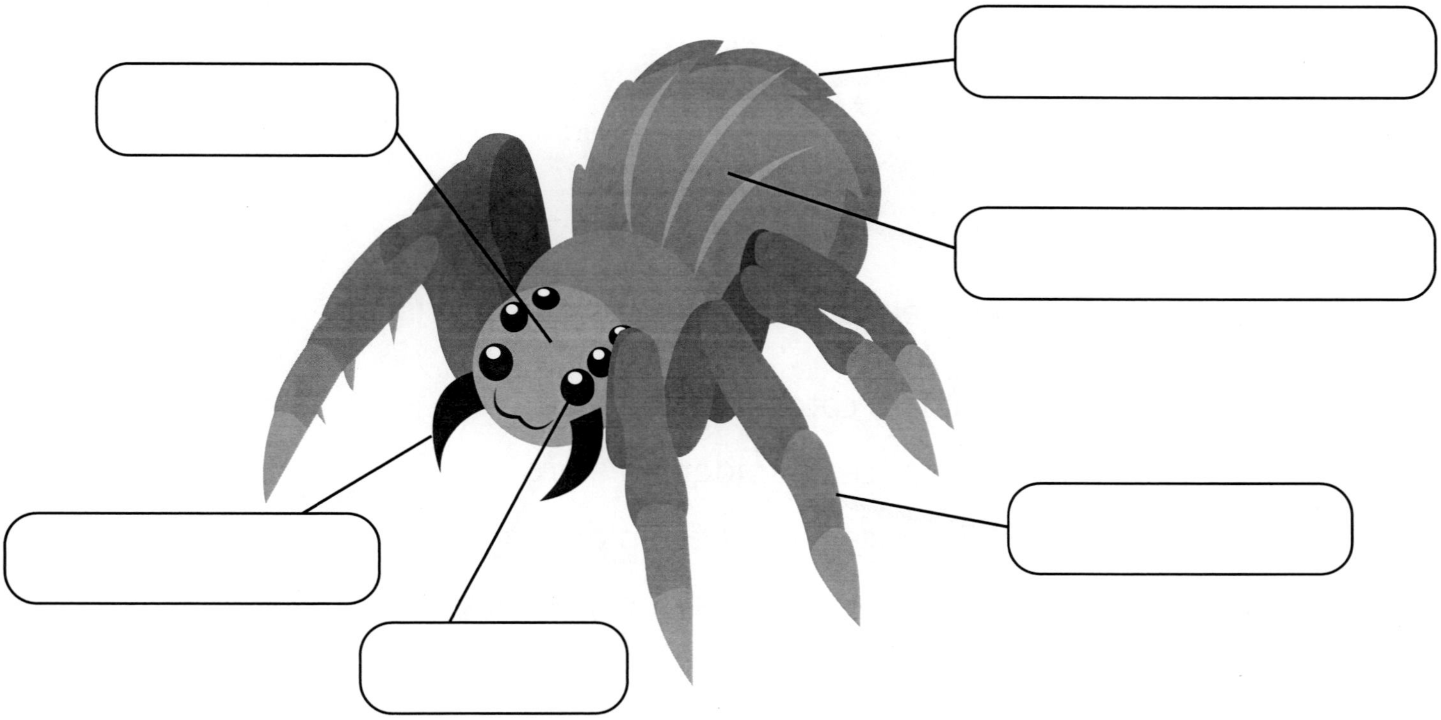

2 Complete the sentence.

The largest kind of spider lives in ______________________ in South America.

A **cause** is what makes something happen.
The **effect** is what happens because of the cause.

3 Write **cause** or **effect** beside the sentence.

a) ___________________: The spider knows an insect is caught in the web.

b) ___________________: The insect tugs at the web as it tries to get away.

Spiders – Think About It! (cont.)

4. When an insect flies into a spider web, why can't the insect escape by walking or flying away?

   a) The spider web is too big.
   b) The spider web is too sticky.
   c) There is poison in the spider web.
   d) The insect is lost and confused.

5. In the "Spider Senses" section, the author's purpose is to...

   a) Explain how spiders catch food
   b) Show the importance of spiders' feelers
   c) Discuss the differences between spiders and insects
   d) Persuade readers to learn about spider senses

6. What are scientists investigating regarding spiders?

   a) How spiders make webs
   b) Ways to protect spiders' habitats
   c) Making new medicines from spiders
   d) Training spiders to do tricks

A **heading** is a title of a section that lets you know what the section is about.

7. Under which heading would you find information on spinnerets?

   a) Spider Webs b) Spider Senses c) Are Spiders Insects?

Spiders – Think About It! (cont.)

8. Write four facts that you learned about spiders.

Unit 13

The Leaf Project

Mark told his mom he had to do a science project about leaves. "Why don't you make a leaf scrapbook?" Mom suggested. "Each page could have a different kind of leaf and a label to tell what kind of leaf it is."

"No, I don't want to do that," said Mark. "That's what lots of kids are doing."

"Well, you could put your leaves in alphabetical order and put the title 'A Leaf Dictionary' on the cover," said Mom.

"That's too much like a scrapbook," said Mark. "I'm going to get a big piece of paper and draw a tree with six branches. Then I'll stick a different kind of leaf on each branch and write a label on each branch."

"Great idea!" replied Mom. "I'll wax the leaves for you. Then they won't dry out and turn brown."

"How will you wax the leaves?" asked Mark.

"I'll put each leaf between two pieces of wax paper, then put two pieces of newspaper on the bottom and top. Then I'll press on each side with a warm iron," Mom explained. "The heat will melt the wax, and the wax will go onto the leaf. The wax will keep the leaf green. Otherwise, it will turn brown."

Mark got an oak leaf and a maple leaf from the trees in his backyard. His mom called the neighbours to find out what kinds of trees they had in their yards. Mark got a poplar leaf and a dogwood leaf from Mrs. Bosco. From Mr. Patel, he got a willow leaf. Mrs. James gave him a beech leaf. Mom waxed all the leaves, then Mark drew a big tree, wrote the label for each leaf, and stuck each waxed leaf on the branch with its label.

When Marks' teacher saw the finished project, she said, "What an interesting way to present the leaves, Mark. Good work!"

The Leaf Project – Think About It!

1. How will Mom wax the leaves for Mark's project?

    a) By painting them with green paint

    b) By using a warm iron to press them between two pieces of wax paper

    c) By putting them in the freezer

    d) By drying them in the sun

2. Draw a line to match the person with what they said in the story.

Mark ●	● "What an interesting way to present the leaves, Mark. Good work!"
Mark's mom ●	● "How will you wax the leaves?"
Mark's teacher ●	● "Why don't you make a leaf scrapbook?"

3. Read each statement and determine whether it is a fact or an opinion. Write ***F*** for fact and ***O*** for opinion.

    a) Mark's mom suggested making a leaf scrapbook. ________

    b) A leaf scrapbook is what lots of kids are doing. ________

    c) Waxing the leaves will keep them from turning brown. ________

    d) Mark's idea of making a tree with six branches is great. ________

    e) Mark's teacher thought his project was interesting. ________

The Leaf Project – Think About It! (cont.)

4 List four kinds of leaves that Mark got from his neighbours.

____

5 Why doesn't Mark want to make a leaf scrapbook for his science project?

a) He thinks it is a better idea to make a leaf dictionary.

b) He thinks making a leaf scrapbook will take too long.

c) He wants his project to be different from other kids' projects.

d) He thinks the project is boring, so he doesn't want to do it.

A **cause** is what makes something happen.
The **effect** is what happens because of the cause.

6 Write **cause** or **effect** beside the sentence.

a) ________________: The leaf stays green instead of turning brown.

b) ________________: An iron is used to melt wax onto a leaf.

7 Complete the sentence.

a) Mark got a ________________ leaf from Mr. Patel.

b) Mrs. James gave Mark a ________________ leaf.

The Leaf Project – Think About It! (cont.)

An **acrostic poem** is a special kind of poem that uses the first letter of each word to spell out a message or a word.

8 Write a leaves acrostic poem. Decorate your poem.

L ______________________________

E ______________________________

A ______________________________

V ______________________________

E ______________________________

S ______________________________

Unit 14

Arctic and Antarctic

Earth is shaped like a giant ball. The area at the top of Earth is called the Arctic. That's where the North Pole is. At the bottom of Earth is an area called the Antarctic. That's where the South Pole is. The Arctic and the Antarctic are both very cold places.

People

Inuit are Indigenous people who have lived in the Arctic for hundreds of years. Long ago, Inuit hunted and fished for food and they lived in snow homes called igloos. Today, airplanes bring food to people who live in the Arctic. Some Inuit still hunt and fish for food.

Igloo

The land in the Antarctic is called Antarctica. No one lives in Antarctica all the time. Scientists go there to learn more about it. They may stay there for months, but their homes are in other places.

Animals

Some animals are able to survive in the frigid winter temperatures of the Arctic and Antarctic. Several kinds of animals live in the Arctic. These include polar bears, caribou (also called reindeer), Arctic foxes, and seals. The Antarctic is home to penguins and seals.

Polar bear

Seasons

From November to February, the Arctic has winter weather. It gets very cold, and the land is covered with ice and snow. Arctic summers last from June to September. The weather is not hot, but it gets warm enough to melt ice and snow. A few plants can grow during the short Arctic summer.

In the Antarctic, the seasons are at opposite times of the year. Summer lasts from October to February, and it is winter from March to September. It can be dangerous for planes to fly to Antarctica in winter because it is so cold that an airplane's fuel might freeze. Then the plane could not fly. Pilots make winter flights to Antarctica only if there is an emergency, such as a scientist who is very sick and needs to go to a hospital. There are no hospitals in Antarctica.

Arctic and Antarctic – Think About It!

1 The text talks about "the frigid winter temperatures" in the Arctic and Antarctic. What does *frigid* mean?

a) Very cold

b) Cool

c) Sometimes cool and sometimes warm

d) Warm

A **cause** is what makes something happen.
The **effect** is what happens because of the cause.

2 Write **cause** or **effect** beside the sentence.

a) ________________: Pilots usually do not fly to Antarctica in winter.

b) ________________: Winter in Antarctica is cold enough to freeze airplane fuel.

3 Complete the sentence.

If you go to Antarctica in June, the season will be ______________.

4 List two animals that live in the Arctic.

____

5 List two animals that live in the Antartic

____

Arctic and Antarctic – Think About It! (cont.)

6. Write each piece of information in the correct box.

- no penguins live there
- penguins live there
- a few plants grow during summer
- is winter in June

Arctic	Antarctic

7. Draw a line to match the vocabulary term with its definition.

Arctic	Area at the bottom of Earth
Antarctic	Homes made of snow
Inuit	Area at the top of Earth
Igloos	Indigenous people who have lived in the Arctic for hundreds of years

8. Decide if the statement is true or false. Write ***T*** for True and ***F*** for False.

a) Earth is shaped like a giant ball. ________

b) The North Pole is found in the Arctic. ________

c) Winter in the Arctic lasts from June to September. ________

d) The Antarctic is home to penguins and seals. ________

Arctic and Antarctic – Think About It! (cont.)

9. Imagine you are a young scientist who has been on an exciting research adventure in either the Arctic or Antarctic. Write an email to a fellow scientist, sharing your experiences and discoveries from your expedition. Use the information provided in the text to help you compose your email.

New Message

To:

From:

Subject:

Hi ______________________________,

____

____

____

____

____

____

From, ______________________________

☐ I used capitals and end marks. ☐ I used linking words to connect my ideas.

☐ I organized my ideas in a way that makes sense. ☐ I used information from the text.

Unit 15 Inside an Animal Shelter

Sometimes, people find a lost dog or cat and take it to an animal shelter. An animal shelter looks after lost animals. People who have lost a pet can go to an animal shelter to find out if someone has brought in their pet.

Vet

When an animal arrives at an animal shelter, a vet checks it to see if it is healthy. If the animal is not healthy, the vet knows how to look after it.

Animal Shelter Workers

Vets and other workers have jobs looking after the animals at an animal shelter. Some workers feed and wash the animals. They also clean the places where the animals live.

Volunteers also work at animal shelters. Some volunteers take dogs for walks or take them to an outdoor area at the shelter where they can run to get exercise. Cats do not go outside, but there is a room where volunteers take them to play. This room might have a climbing wall so the cats can get exercise by jumping and climbing. Both cats and dogs need exercise. They also need lots of love and attention from humans. Volunteers help make sure the dogs and cats get the exercise and attention they need.

Shelter volunteers

Adopting Animals

People who have lost a dog or cat might find it at an animal shelter. If a pet's owner does not come looking for their pet, the animal shelter will let someone else adopt it. Animal shelter workers and volunteers are thrilled every time an animal is picked up by its owner or is adopted. These people know that the best life for a dog or cat is in a home with people who love it.

Adopting a new cat

Inside an Animal Shelter – Think About It!

A **text** is a piece of writing that you can read.
The **main idea** is what the text is mostly about.

1. What is the main idea of the text?

    a) Volunteers help provide exercise and attention to animals in shelters.
    b) Vets and workers play important roles in animal shelters.
    c) Animal shelters provide care and shelter for lost animals.
    d) Animal shelters help with the adoption of lost dogs and cats.

2. Workers and volunteers are thrilled when animals leave the shelter. What does *thrilled* mean?

    a) Sad and disappointed
    b) Happy and excited
    c) Very busy
    d) A bit nervous

3. Complete the sentence.

    People can go to an animal shelter to ____________________ a new pet to take home.

4. Under which heading would you find information about what happens if a pet owner does not come looking for their pet?

    a) Animal Shelter Workers
    b) Adopting Animals

Inside an Animal Shelter – Think About It! (cont.)

5. Read the statement carefully. Determine whether the statement is true or false. Circle your answer.

a) T F Animal shelters provide care and support for lost animals.

b) T F Vets at animal shelters only check the health of animals if they are sick.

c) T F Volunteers at animal shelters help dogs and cats get the exercise they need.

d) T F Animal shelters allow anyone to adopt a pet without checking if someone lost the pet first.

6. If you were a volunteer at an animal shelter, what tasks would you like to help with?

____

____

7. Choose the best opening sentence for the following paragraph.

______________________________ Workers and volunteers give them food, baths, and playtime. They make sure the animals are healthy and happy until they find a loving family to adopt them. Animal shelters help animals and bring joy to their lives!

a) Workers and volunteers spend time with animals.

b) Animal shelters are special places where lost animals are taken care of.

Inside an Animal Shelter – Think About It! (cont.)

A **slogan** is a catchy phrase that helps people remember an important idea.

8. Design a poster with a catchy slogan to inspire people to adopt pets from animal shelters. Use information from the text and your own ideas.

☐ I created a slogan that encourages people to adopt pets from animal shelters.

☐ I included other important details in the text.

Unit 16 Mighty Moose vs. Terrific Tigers

Once upon a time, in a hockey rink far, far away, there was an incredible game about to begin. The teams were the Mighty Moose and the Terrific Tigers. The Mighty Moose were known for their lightning-fast skating, while the Terrific Tigers had a goalie with cat-like reflexes.

As the game started, the puck dropped and the players zoomed across the ice like shooting stars. The Mighty Moose were as strong as bears, shooting powerful shots at the goalie. But the goalie was like a brick wall, easily stopping every shot.

Then, something extraordinary happened. The Mighty Moose player named Max had a magical hockey stick that made the puck as slippery as a fish. Every time Max touched the puck, it danced and swirled like a tornado, confusing the Terrific Tigers.

But the Tigers weren't about to give up. Their captain, Sam, had a rocket-powered helmet that made him zoom across the ice like a superhero. He dodged and weaved through the Moose players, scoring goal after goal.

The crowd cheered with excitement as the game became more and more intense. The players showed off their incredible skills, making passes as smooth as melted chocolate and saves as solid as a fortress.

The game was like a wild roller coaster ride, filled with twists and turns, laughter and cheers. In the end, both teams played their hearts out, and the final score was a tie.

And so, the Mighty Moose and the Terrific Tigers shook hands and celebrated their amazing game, knowing they were all winners. The hockey rink was filled with joy, and the story of that incredible game would be told for years to come.

Mighty Moose vs. Terrific Tigers – Think About It!

1. What is the main purpose of this story?

   a) To inform readers about the rules of hockey

   b) To entertain readers with an exciting hockey game

   c) To persuade readers to play hockey

   d) To describe different types of sports

2. Which team had a goalie with cat-like reflexes?

   a) Mighty Moose   b) Terrific Tigers

3. How does comparing the goalie to a brick wall make you think about the goalie?

   a) It shows that the goalie is fast.

   b) It shows that the goalie is good at moving.

   c) It shows that the goalie can stop shots easily.

4. The puck glides across the ice as smooth as a swan. The word *glides* means

   a) slides smoothly   b) jumps   c) stops suddenly

5. How did the game end?

   a) The Mighty Moose won.   b) It was a tie.

A **caption** tells what a picture is about.

6. Write a caption for the picture in the text.

Mighty Moose vs. Terrific Tigers – Think About It! (cont.)

7. How did the Terrific Tigers score their goals?

   a) By using a rocket-powered helmet

   b) By shooting powerful shots at the goalie

   c) By confusing the Mighty Moose players

A **simile** is a form of descriptive writing that compares two unlike things using the words ***like*** or ***as***.

8. Draw a line to match the simile used in the text with its meaning.

Like shooting stars	Moving in twists and turns
Slippery as a fish	Strong and hard to get past
Danced and swirled like a tornado	Moving very fast
Saves as solid as a fortress	Very smooth and hard to catch

9. Fill in the blank with your own suitable simile.

   a) The players skate across the ice as swift as ______________________________.

   b) The game is full of surprises, just like ______________________________.

   c) The goalie is like ______________________________ protecting the net.

   d) The puck glides across the ice as smooth as ______________________________.

Mighty Moose vs. Terrific Tigers – Think About It! (cont.)

10. Imagine you have the power to create your own superhero hockey player. Describe your superheroes' special abilities and how they help the team. **Challenge:** Include at least three similes in your writing.

Draw a picture.

- [ ] I used capitals and end marks.
- [ ] I used linking words to connect my ideas.
- [ ] I organized my ideas in a way that makes sense.
- [ ] I included three similes.

Unit 17

The Eiffel Tower

One of the most famous towers in the world is the Eiffel Tower (say Eiffel like this: eye-full). It is in the city of Paris in France. The Eiffel Tower is a place most people want to go to on their first visit to Paris. There are usually long lineups to go up the tower.

The Eiffel Tower is more than 130 years old.

When the tower was built, it was the tallest building in the world.

The Eiffel Tower is built of metal to make it strong.

The bottom of the tower is much wider than the top. The wide bottom part helps keep strong wind from pushing the tower over.

The tower has three platforms, or floors, where people can go.

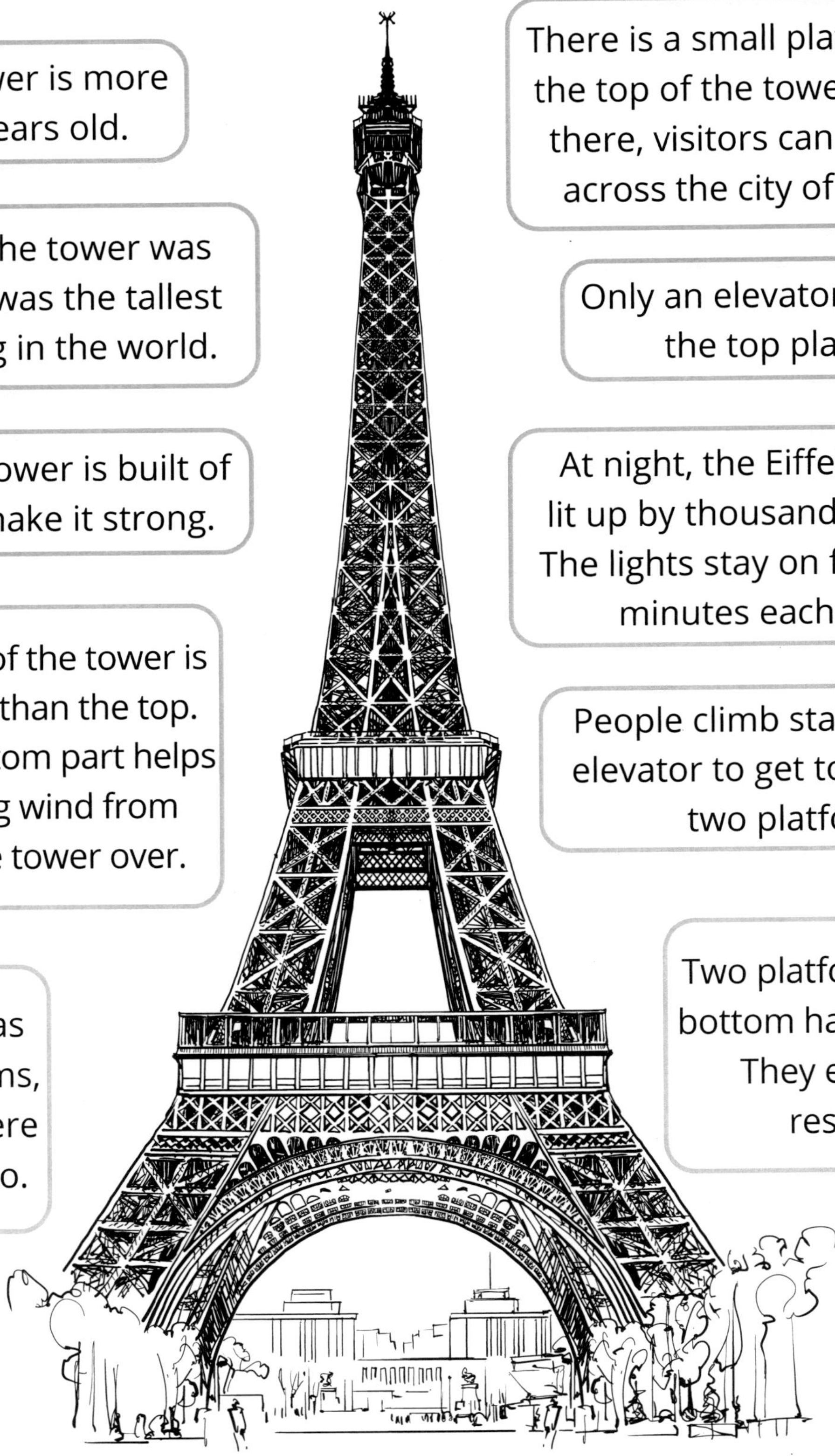

There is a small platform at the top of the tower. From there, visitors can see all across the city of Paris.

Only an elevator goes up to the top platform.

At night, the Eiffel Tower is lit up by thousands of lights. The lights stay on for just five minutes each hour.

People climb stairs or use an elevator to get to the bottom two platforms.

Two platforms are in the bottom half of the tower. They each have a restaurant.

The Eiffel Tower – Think About It!

1. What is one reason why so many people who visit Paris want to go to the Eiffel Tower?

   a) It is made of metal.
   b) It is narrow at the top.
   c) It has an elevator.
   d) It is a very famous tower.

2. Complete the sentence.

   At night, the lights on the Eiffel Tower stay on for ____________ minutes each hour.

A **cause** is what makes something happen.
The **effect** is what happens because of the cause.

3. Write **cause** or **effect** beside the sentence.

   a) ________________: Strong wind does not push the tower over.

   b) ________________: The tower was built to be wider at the bottom.

4. Write each piece of information in the correct box.

   - use stairs or elevator to get there
   - must use an elevator to get there
   - widest part
   - narrowest part

Top of the Eiffel Tower	Bottom of the Eiffel Tower

The Eiffel Tower – Think About It! (cont.)

5 Read the statement carefully. Determine whether the statement is true or false. Circle your answer.

a) T F The Eiffel Tower is located in the city of Paris, France.

b) T F The Eiffel Tower is the tallest building in the world.

c) T F The Eiffel Tower is more than 130 years old.

d) T F The bottom part of the Eiffel Tower is wider than the top to help withstand strong winds.

e) T F There are three platforms or floors in the Eiffel Tower where people can go.

f) T F Both platforms in the bottom half of the tower have restaurants.

g) T F Visitors can only use an elevator to reach the top platform of the Eiffel Tower.

h) T F At night, the Eiffel Tower is lit up by thousands of lights.

i) T F The lights on the Eiffel Tower stay on all the time.

j) T F From the top platform of the Eiffel Tower, people can see all across Paris.

The Eiffel Tower – Think About It! (cont.)

6 At night, the Eiffel Tower lights up with thousands of lights, and it looks absolutely beautiful! Pretend you are visiting at night and create a post.

☐ I used capitals and end marks. ☐ My printing is neat. ☐ My writing makes sense.

Unit 18

Three Kinds of Bees

Bees live in homes called hives. Many thousands of bees live in one hive. A group of bees that lives in one hive is called a colony. Every colony has three kinds of bees.

Queen Bee

Each colony of bees has only one queen bee. The queen is larger than the other bees. Her only job is to lay eggs, and she can lay up to 2000 eggs in one day.

Queen bee

Worker Bees

A colony has thousands of worker bees. All worker bees are female. They got their name because they do all the work, except laying eggs. The many jobs of a worker bee include collecting nectar and pollen from flowers, feeding the queen bee, looking after the babies that hatch, and keeping the hive clean.

Worker bee

Worker bees also keep the inside of the hive at the right temperature. When the hive gets too warm, worker bees go to the entrance of the hive and flap their wings. Their wings act like fans and push out the warm air. In cold weather, worker bees inside the hive flap their wings, shiver, and wiggle their bodies. All this activity makes their bodies warmer. The heat from their bodies warms up the hive.

Drones

The hundreds of male bees in a colony are called drones. The drones are about the same size as workers, but drones have much bigger eyes. Drones are the only bees in a colony that do not have stingers.

Drone

A drone's job is to fly around, find a queen bee from another colony, and be her mate. Once the queen bee has a mate, she can start to lay eggs in her own hive.

In fall, worker bees force all the drones to leave the hive. The drones die. New drones will hatch from some of the eggs the queen has laid.

Three Kinds of Bees – Think About It!

1. Complete the sentence.

   A group of bees living in one hive is called a ___________________.

2. What is the main job of the queen bee?

   a) Collecting food from flowers
   b) Building the hive
   c) Laying eggs
   d) Guarding the hive

3. Why are some bees called *worker* bees?

   a) They protect the hive from danger.
   b) They do all the important tasks in the hive, except laying eggs.
   c) They fly around to find nectar.
   d) They make honey.

4. How do worker bees help keep the hive at the right temperature?

   a) They fan their wings to cool it down or wiggle to warm it up.
   b) They gather pollen to feed the queen bee.
   c) They collect nectar from flowers.
   d) They build new hive cells.

5. Imagine you are a worker bee. Design a new task that you could do in the hive to help the colony. Explain your idea.

   ____

   ____

Three Kinds of Bees – Think About It! (cont.)

6 Write each piece of information in the correct box.

- all male
- control temperature
- lay eggs
- are mates for the queen
- hundreds in a colony
- largest bees
- no stingers
- collect nectar and pollen
- thousands in a colony
- feed the queen bee

Queen Bees	
Worker Bees	
Drones	

Three Kinds of Bees – Think About It! (cont.)

7. **Haiku** is a traditional style of Japanese poetry. Usually, haiku poems have a nature theme, such as animals or the seasons.

Haiku poems have only three lines with an exact number of syllables.

Line 1 is 5 syllables
Line 2 is 7 syllables
Line 3 is 5 syllables

For example:

Leaves blow in the wind
Skies darken and thunder booms.
The rain helps things grow.

Brainstorm a list of words about bees. Write the number of syllables.

Write a haiku poem about bees.

Unit 19 Convincing People to Buy a Product

Advertising tries to convince people to buy the product that is advertised. What are some ways that advertising tries to do this?

Give Facts About the Product

A fact is a piece of information that is always true. Here is an example of a fact: Yummy Crunch cereal is made from wheat. The company that makes this cereal can prove that it is always made from wheat. This is a fact because it is always true.

Give Opinions About the Product

Nick says: "Mmmmm. This is the BEST cake I have ever had!"

Bakery's Own Cakes the best you will ever have!

An opinion is a piece of information that is true for some people, but not for everyone. Here is an example of an opinion: Yummy Crunch is the best cereal I have ever tasted. Some people might agree that Yummy Crunch is the best cereal they have ever tasted. Other people might think that another type of cereal tastes better. The opinion that Yummy Crunch tastes best is not true for everyone.

Compare the Product to Similar Products

Imagine that you have created a new cereal called Tasty Bites. You want to convince people to buy your cereal instead of Yummy Crunch. Your advertising could compare Tasty Bites to Yummy Crunch.

Here are two examples:
- Tasty Bites has more vitamins than Yummy Crunch.
- Tasty Bites has a toy inside but Yummy Crunch does not.

Convincing People to Buy a Product – Think About It!

1. What is the author's main purpose in writing this text?

   a) To entertain readers with a story about cereal
   b) To persuade readers to buy Yummy Crunch cereal
   c) To inform readers about how advertising can convince people to buy a product

2. What is advertising?

   ____

3. Which of the following is a fact about Yummy Crunch cereal?

   a) Yummy Crunch is made from wheat.
   b) Yummy Crunch is the best cereal ever.
   c) Yummy Crunch has a toy inside.

4. What does it mean if something is an opinion?

   a) It is always true.
   b) It is true for some people, but not for everyone.
   c) It can be proven by the company.

5. If you wanted to show that Tasty Bites is better than Yummy Crunch, what could you do in your advertising?

   a) Say that Tasty Bites is made from wheat.
   b) Compare Tasty Bites to Yummy Crunch, like saying Tasty Bites has more vitamins.
   c) Say that Yummy Crunch is the best cereal ever.

Convincing People to Buy a Product – Think About It! (cont.)

6 Write ***fact*** if the sentence is true and can be proven.
Write ***opinion*** if the sentence is a personal belief or feeling.

a) ______________ Super Fast running shoes come in four different colours.

b) ______________ You will love your new Super Fast running shoes.

c) ______________ Your whole family will enjoy playing the Race to Win board game.

d) ______________ Race to Win comes with four game pieces and two dice.

7 Think of a product that you or your family have bought. Give one fact and one opinion about the product.

Name of Product

Fact About the Product	Opinion About the Product

Convincing People to Buy a Product – Think About It! (cont.)

8 Let's imagine you've just invented a brand new cereal! Now, it's your job to create an advertisement that will make everyone want to try it.

Make sure to include the following:

- cereal name
- what makes your cereal special
- catchy slogan or phrase
- fun character or mascot

9 In what ways does your ad make children want to try your new cereal?

Amazing Stories

What Is Real in Stories?

Books are not the only places where we find stories. Movies and television shows tell stories, too. Amazing things happen in many stories.

Sometimes stories tell us about things that could really happen. You might read a story about a girl who finds a buried treasure. That could really happen. Sometimes people really do find buried treasure.

You might also see a movie about a boy who can make himself invisible. In real life, people cannot make themselves invisible. Sometimes things happen in stories that cannot happen in real life.

Use Your Imagination

People use their imaginations to create interesting stories. You could write a story about a place where all the trees are blue. There is no such place in real life, but it might be fun to write a story about it.

You could write a story about strange monsters with purple fur. In real life, there are no monsters with purple fur. When you write a story, you can use your imagination to write about things that are not real.

People use their imaginations to create the stories we see in books, television shows, and movies. Some stories are about things that are not real. In a story, anything can happen!

Amazing Stories – Think About It!

1. Where else, besides books, can we find stories?

   a) In songs b) In movies and television shows
   c) In paintings d) In dreams

2. Read the statement carefully. Determine whether the statement is true or false. Circle your answer.

   a) T F People sometimes find buried treasure in real life.

   b) T F In real life, there are monsters with purple fur.

   c) T F You can only write stories about things that are real.

   d) T F All the trees are blue in some places.

   e) T F Anything can happen in a story.

3. Draw a line to match the word with its meaning.

Buried Treasure	Not able to be seen
Imagination	The ability to think of new ideas or pictures in your mind
Monsters	Something very valuable that is hidden underground
Invisible	Imaginary creatures that are often scary

Amazing Stories – Think About It! (cont.)

4. In a fairy tale, a boy plants a seed. The seed grows into a plant that is so tall it touches the sky.

   Put a **check mark** beside the things that could happen in real life.
   Put an **X** beside things that could not happen in real life.

   a) __________ A boy plants a seed.

   b) __________ The seed grows into a plant.

   c) __________ The plant grows so tall that it touches the sky.

> On a television show, a girl gets a toy robot for her birthday. She gets the robot to do her homework for her. Then her cat climbs onto her desk. The cat says, "You should not let the robot do your homework for you!"

5. Write two things from the television show that could really happen.

____

____

____

6. Write two things from the television show that could not really happen.

____

____

____

Amazing Stories – Think About It! (cont.)

Read or listen to a story, or watch a movie or television show. Write which things could happen in real life, and which things could not.

7 I am writing about:

☐ a story I read or listened to ☐ a television show ☐ a movie

Title: ______________________________

a) Things that could happen in real life:

____

____

____

____

b) Things that could not happen in real life:

____

____

____

____

☐ I used capitals and end marks. ☐ I used linking words to connect my ideas.

☐ I organized my ideas in a way that makes sense.

Unit 21

David Suzuki

David Suzuki is a Canadian scientist. He became famous for helping Canadians learn more about science. He teaches people about nature and how they can help to protect the environment.

David is a Japanese Canadian. A Japanese Canadian is someone who is a Canadian citizen and has ancestors from Japan.

Growing Up

David was born in 1936 in Vancouver, British Columbia. Later, David's family moved to Ontario. After high school, David went to university in the United States to become a scientist. Then he returned to Canada and taught at a university in British Columbia.

Teaching People About Nature

When David was young, his father helped him to become interested in nature. As a scientist, David learned more about nature and the environment. He saw that people can help or hurt nature. He wanted to share his knowledge with people who were not scientists.

In 1970, David started a television show about science for kids. Four years later, he started a radio show about science for adults. He went on to create many more television shows about science and nature. Some of these television shows won awards and were seen in countries around the world.

David has written more than 50 books about science, including many books for kids. His books and television shows teach people that it is important to care about nature. They also tell people what they can do to help protect nature and the environment.

David Suzuki – Think About It!

1. What is David Suzuki famous for?

    a) Helping Canadians learn about science
    b) Teaching people about art
    c) Playing sports professionally

2. Where was David Suzuki born?

    a) Toronto, Ontario
    b) Vancouver, British Columbia
    c) Montreal, Quebec

3. What did David Suzuki's father help him become interested in?

    a) Science and nature   b) Music and dance   c) Cooking and baking

4. What did David Suzuki start in 1970?

    a) A newspaper about the environment
    b) A radio show about animals
    c) A television show about science for kids

5. How many books has David Suzuki written?

    a) Only 5   b) None   c) More than 50

6. Why do you think it's important for everyone to learn about nature and how to protect the environment?

____

David Suzuki – Think About It! (cont.)

7 Match the following words with their meanings.

Japanese Canadian		Someone who studies the natural world and its phenomena.
Scientist		Someone who helps protect nature and the environment.
Nature		The surroundings in which living beings exist.
Environment		A person who is a Canadian citizen with ancestors from Japan.
Environmentalist		The world of plants, animals, and the physical features of Earth.

8 Complete the word search. Circle the words as you find them.

W	Y	C	S	U	Z	U	K	I
B	J	A	P	A	N	E	S	E
O	V	N	R	X	Q	T	M	E
O	G	A	O	I	R	P	Z	R
K	Y	D	T	B	Q	N	O	U
S	C	I	E	N	T	I	S	T
U	I	A	C	A	R	E	N	A
V	W	N	T	X	H	P	L	N

Words to search for:

books
Canadian
care
Japanese
nature
protect
scientist
Suzuki

David Suzuki – Think About It! (cont.)

An **interview** is a conversation between two people.
One person (the interviewer) asks questions.
The other person (the interviewee) answers those questions.

9 Pretend you are going to interview David Suzuki.

What are three questions you would ask him?

____

____

____

____

____

____

Draw a picture.

☐ I used capitals and end marks. ☐ I used linking words to connect my ideas.

☐ I organized my ideas in a way that makes sense.

Unit 22

Fluffy

Meet my pet rabbit, Fluffy! Fluffy is a small, cuddly animal with soft, snow-white fur that feels like a cloud when you touch it. Her ears are long and stand straight up when she hears a sound. They feel like velvet when you pet them.

Fluffy has big, round eyes that are a beautiful shade of blue, like the sky on a clear day. When she looks at you, it feels like she understands everything. Her little pink nose is always twitching, sniffing out treats like carrots and lettuce.

Her body is small and round, perfect for snuggling. She has four little paws with tiny claws, which she uses to hop around quickly. But don't worry, she's very gentle and never scratches.

Fluffy lives in a large wooden hutch in our backyard. It has a cozy sleeping area filled with hay where she loves to nap during the day. Fluffy also has a large play area where she can hop around, eat her food, and play with her favourite toys.

Fluffy is a very playful pet. She loves to hop around the yard, especially early in the morning when the grass is still covered in dew. She also enjoys playing with her little toy ball, pushing it around with her nose.

Even though Fluffy can't talk, she communicates in a special way. When she's happy, she'll do a funny little hop and twist in the air, called a "binky." And she'll nudge your leg with her nose when she wants attention. Fluffy is the best pet ever, and I love her so much!

Fluffy – Think About It!

1. Why did the author write this passage about Fluffy?

   a) To convince us to buy a rabbit
   b) To tell us a story about a rabbit
   c) To describe what Fluffy the rabbit is like
   d) To explain how to take care of a rabbit

2. When the author says Fluffy's fur feels like a "cloud," what do they mean?

   a) Fluffy's fur is white.
   b) Fluffy's fur is soft.
   c) Fluffy's fur is wet.
   d) Fluffy's fur is dark.

3. Based on the text, how does the author probably feel about Fluffy?

   a) The author is scared of Fluffy.
   b) The author is annoyed by Fluffy.
   c) The author loves Fluffy.
   d) The author is does not care about Fluffy.

4. What does the word "hutch" mean in this text?

   a) A small house for a rabbit
   b) A type of food
   c) A type of toy
   d) A big yard

5. What does it mean when Fluffy does a "binky"?

   a) She is hungry.
   b) She is bored.
   c) She is happy.
   d) She is tired.

Fluffy – Think About It! (cont.)

6. Fill in the chart with character traits of Fluffy.

On the Outside (Physical Traits)

This is what we can see with our eyes.

Portrait

On the Inside (Personality Traits)

This is what we learn based on what the character says, does, and feels.

Fluffy – Think About It! (cont.)

A **simile poem** contains similes to compare and describe an object or action. Similes use the words ***like*** or ***as*** to compare.

For example:

The sun is like a golden ball,
High up in the sky so tall,
It shines so bright for all to see,
Like a giant lamp, it lights our day with glee.

7. Write your own simile poem. Decorate your poem.

Unit 23 Johnny's Magical Adventures

Once upon a time, a boy named Johnny lived in a little town called Sunnyville. Johnny had a head full of dreams as big as a giant's castle and a heart as wild as a stampeding herd of horses. People in the town said he had a magic touch, and everything he did became an adventure!

One day, as Johnny was walking through the forest, he stumbled upon a river as wide as an ocean. The water roared like a lion, challenging anyone to cross it. Johnny, being as brave as a knight, shouted, "I will conquer this mighty river!"

With a leap as high as a kangaroo, Johnny jumped onto a floating log and paddled across the river faster than a cheetah. The log carried him like a magic carpet, sailing as smooth as silk through the water.

As Johnny reached the other side, he came across a mountain taller than any he had ever seen. With muscles as strong as a bear's, he easily climbed to the top. From there, he could see the whole town, looking as small as tiny ants. "I am the king of the world!" Johnny exclaimed, his voice echoing like thunder.

Johnny's adventures continued as he discovered a cave filled with treasures as shiny as a shooting star. With pockets as deep as the ocean, he collected gold and jewels, enough to fill a pirate's treasure chest.

Word of Johnny's magical adventures spread far and wide like wildfire in the night. People came from near and far, hoping to witness his incredible feats. But, instead, they called him the "Fearless Explorer" and marvelled at his incredible talents.

But Johnny, as humble as a gentle breeze, knew it was all in good fun. He cherished his tall tales and shared them with everyone, making them laugh and smile.

Johnny's Magical Adventures – Think About It!

A **tall tale** is a funny and exciting story that tells exaggerated adventures about larger-than-life characters.

1 Use the word box to fill in the blank for the simile sentence.

breeze	feats	giant	kangaroo
laugh	lion	magic	wide

a) Johnny had dreams as big as a _______________'s castle.

b) The water roared like a _______________, challenging anyone to cross it.

c) With a leap as high as a _______________, Johnny jumped onto a floating log.

d) People in town said he had a _______________ touch.

e) Word of Johnny's magical adventures spread far and _______________.

f) People came from near and far, hoping to witness his incredible _______________.

g) But Johnny, as humble as a gentle _______________, knew it was all in good fun.

h) He cherished his tall tales and shared them with everyone, making them _______________ and smile.

Johnny's Magical Adventures – Think About It! (cont.)

2. List three similes from the text.

____

____

____

Hyperbole is when we use big exaggerations to make things sound really funny or exciting. *Example: my backpack weighs a ton.*

3. Read each sentence and complete the hyperbole by filling in the blank with your own words. Use your imagination to come up with creative and exaggerated descriptions.

a) Johnny had dreams as big as a __________'s castle.

Your Completion: ______________________________

b) The water roared like a __________, challenging anyone to cross it.

Your Completion: ______________________________

c) With a leap as high as a __________, Johnny jumped onto a floating log.

Your Completion: ______________________________

d) Johnny's adventures continued as he discovered a cave filled with treasures as shiny as a __________.

Your Completion: ______________________________

Johnny's Magical Adventures – Think About It! (cont.)

4. Did you like the story? Explain your thinking.

Draw a picture of your favourite part. Include a caption.

☐ I used capitals and end marks. ☐ I used linking words to connect my ideas.

☐ I organized my ideas in a way that makes sense.

Unit 24

Cree Powwow

One bright Saturday, my family and I were buzzing with excitement. We were going to the big Cree Powwow in our town in Saskatchewan.

Dancer wearing regalia

As we drove, I saw wide golden fields under the bright blue sky. My little sister was bouncing in her seat. She couldn't wait to see the dancers in their beautiful regalia.

When we arrived, everyone was smiling and laughing. I felt a warm glow inside. I was proud to be Cree, proud of our songs, our dances, and our stories.

My little sister and I watched the dancers spin and leap. Their regalia were a whirl of colours. Some had shiny beads and others had feathers that fluttered as they danced. The dancers' regalia are like special decorated clothing that people wear for special occasions. The regalia made the dancers look like they were swirling and twirling in a magical way.

I felt the rhythm in my chest. It was like my heart was dancing along with the beat. The smell of delicious bannock filled the air.

Later, we sat with our family and ate bannock and stew. We listened to the Elders tell stories about our ancestors. I felt happy and proud. It was a day I would remember always—a day of celebrating being Cree.

Cree Powwow – Think About It!

1 Draw a line to match the vocabulary word with its correct definition.

Powwow	The beat or pattern of music that makes you want to move and dance.
Regalia	Wise and respected members of the community who have lots of knowledge and experience to share.
Rhythm	Our family members who lived a long time ago, like our grandparents and great-grandparents.
Bannock	A special event where Indigenous people celebrate their culture through dance, music, and storytelling.
Elders	A group of Indigenous people who share the same customs, traditions, and history.
Ancestors	Special decorated clothing worn during important events or ceremonies.
Cree	A kind of bread that is cooked over a fire and is a traditional food of Indigenous people.

Cree Powwow – Think About It! (cont.)

2. What is the main purpose of a powwow?

   a) To celebrate culture and traditions
   b) To have a picnic
   c) To play games
   d) To watch movies

3. How did the narrator feel when they arrived at the powwow?

   a) Bored
   b) Scared
   c) Excited
   d) Sad

4. How can you show pride in your own culture?

   a) By learning traditional dances
   b) By wearing special clothing
   c) By sharing stories and songs
   d) All of the above

5. How do the dancers' regalia make the powwow more exciting?

   a) They make people sing
   b) They add bright colors and make it lively
   c) They help the dancers jump higher
   d) They tell stories about nature

6. Why is it important to learn about our ancestors?

   a) They are famous people in history
   b) They can teach us important lessons and values
   c) They give us presents on special occasions
   d) They lived in different countries

Cree Powwow – Think About It! (cont.)

7. Imagine you are going to a celebration or special event for your own culture. Draw and colour a picture of the special clothing you would wear.

Write a description of your clothing and explain the importance of each part.

☐ I used capitals and end marks. ☐ I used linking words to connect my ideas.

☐ I organized my ideas in a way that makes sense.

Reading Challenge

Colour the box as you finish reading that kind of text.

a book of poetry	a fairy tale	a book that teaches a lesson about life	a book with animals
a book that is part of a series	a magazine	a book that you read outside of class	realistic fiction
a book that teaches you how to do something	a book with a mystery	a book recommended by a friend	a book with an adventure
a non-fiction book	a fantasy	a story about a real person's life	a book you have read outloud to someone else
a chapter book	a picture book	an online article	a graphic novel or comic book

Reading Log – Books I Have Read

Book Title	Purpose of the Text	Rate This Book
	☐ to inform ☐ to entertain ☐ to persuade	☆ ☆ ☆ ☆
	☐ to inform ☐ to entertain ☐ to persuade	☆ ☆ ☆ ☆
	☐ to inform ☐ to entertain ☐ to persuade	☆ ☆ ☆ ☆
	☐ to inform ☐ to entertain ☐ to persuade	☆ ☆ ☆ ☆
	☐ to inform ☐ to entertain ☐ to persuade	☆ ☆ ☆ ☆
	☐ to inform ☐ to entertain ☐ to persuade	☆ ☆ ☆ ☆

Making Connections (text-to-self)

Learning Goal: I understand what I'm reading by making connections between the text and my own experiences.

Choose a Sentence Starter:

☐ The text reminds me of similarities in or differences between

- my life, family, and friends
- places I have been
- experiences I have had

Making Connections (text-to-text)

Learning Goal: I can connect what I am reading to something else that I have read in the past.

Choose a Sentence Starter:

☐ How is text the similar to or different from another text?

Consider:

- genre
- character
- theme
- setting
- plot

Making Connections (text-to-world)

Learning Goal: I can connect what I am reading to something that is happening, or something that has happened in the world.

Choose a Sentence Starter:

☐ This text reminds me of similarities in or differences between

- something I have seen or heard in the media
- historical events or current events

That Reminds Me

Title: ______________________________

This book reminds me of: ☐ something else I have read ☐ something about me ☐ the world around me

Let me tell you why.

____

____

____

____

____

____

☐ I used capitals and end marks. ☐ My printing is neat. ☐ My writing makes sense.

Reading Response

Title: ______________________________

This book is: ☐ Fiction ☐ Non-Fiction

RATE THIS BOOK

☆☆☆☆

Draw a picture of your favourite part of the book.

This is my favourite part of the book. Let me tell you why.

____

____

____

____

____

____

____

☐ I used capitals and end marks. ☐ My printing is neat. ☐ My writing makes sense.

Book Review

Title: ____

Author: ____________________________

MY RATING

☆ ☆ ☆ ☆

Author purpose: ☐ to inform ☐ to entertain ☐ to persuade

What was the book about?

____

____

____

Do you think other people would like the book? Explain your thinking.

____

____

____

Would you tell a friend to read the book? Why or why not?

____

☐ I used capitals and end marks. ☐ My printing is neat. ☐ My writing makes sense.

Hyperboles

Hyperbole is a writing technique that uses big exaggerations to make things sound really funny or exciting. *Example: My backpack weighs a ton!*

1 Draw the hyperbole.

My shoes are killing me!

I have a million things to do today!

2 Write your own hyperbole on the line. Then draw the hyperbole.

Alliteration

Alliterations are sentences or phrases that contain words that repeat the same beginning word sound.
Example: Funny frogs flip and flop on the forest floor.

1. Use the word box to fill in the blank for the alliteration sentence.

dances	jumps	Katie	paper	red

a) Randy rode his ______________ bike rapidly down the road.

b) ______________ kept the key in her pocket for safekeeping.

c) Danny's dog ______________ delightfully during dinnertime.

d) Penny painted pretty pink petals on her ______________.

e) Jenny ______________ joyfully on the jungle gym.

2. Create some of your own examples of **alliteration** below.

a) ____

b) ____

c) ____

d) ____

Idioms

An **idiom** is a phrase that doesn't mean what it seems to mean. It has a special meaning that is different from the way it sounds.

1. Draw a line to match the idiom with its meaning.

Break a leg	To be silent or unable to speak
Piece of cake	To be in trouble or facing a difficult situation
Cat got your tongue?	To be very easy
Add insult to injury	To say something that is exactly right
Butterflies in my stomach	To perform well or have good luck
In hot water	To make a difficult situation even worse
Hit the nail on the head	To feel very happy
On cloud nine	To feel very nervous or scared

Title: ______________________________

☐ I used capitals and end marks. ☐ My printing is neat. ☐ My writing makes sense.

Recount Writing Planner

Who?

What?

When?

Where?

Why?

My Recount About a Visit!

A **recount text pattern** is a type of writing that tells about something that happened, often in the order it happened, with details and sometimes personal thoughts or feelings.

Write a recount of a visit you made to a special place.
Draw the place on a separate piece of paper.

____

____

____

____

____

____

____

____

____

____

____

____

- ☐ I told the order of events with words like *first, next, then, before, after,* and *finally*.
- ☐ I ordered my ideas in a way that makes sense.
- ☐ I used *I* or *we* in my writing.
- ☐ I made sure to include details that answer *who, what, where, when*, and *why*.
- ☐ I checked that my spelling and punctuation were correct.

Fact and Opinion

I read about this topic: ____

✓ **Fact** A statement that can be proven to be true.
Opinion A feeling or belief about something.

☐ I used capitals and end marks. ☐ My printing is neat. ☐ My writing makes sense.

What Is Your Opinion?

An **opinion** is a person's belief or feeling about a topic.

Opinion sentence starters:

- I prefer...
- I believe...
- I think...
- I feel...
- The best thing about...
- The worst part about...
- Everyone should...
- I agree/disagree with...

State your opinion: ____

____

First of all, ____

____

____

____

Another reason ____

____

____

____

Also, ____

____

____

____

This is why I think ____

☐ I used capitals and end marks. ☐ My printing is neat. ☐ My writing makes sense.

Exploring Persuasive Writing

Persuasive writing gives your opinion and tries to convince the reader to agree with you.

Read the statement below. Write a persuasive paragraph to convince the reader of your opinion. Make sure to add details to support your thinking.

"Kids should have a set bedtime."

I (agree, disagree) that kids should have a set bedtime.

First of all, ____

____

____

____

Another reason ____

____

____

____

Also, ____

____

____

____

This is why I think ____

☐ I used capitals and end marks. ☐ My printing is neat. ☐ My writing makes sense.

Exploring More Persuasive Writing

Persuasive writing gives your opinion and tries to convince the reader to agree with you.

Read the statement below. Write a persuasive paragraph to convince the reader of your opinion. Make sure to add details to support your thinking.

"Pets should be allowed in school."

I (agree, disagree) that pets should be allowed in school.

First of all, ____

____

____

____

Another reason ____

____

____

____

Also, ____

____

____

____

This is why I think ____

☐ I used capitals and end marks. ☐ My printing is neat. ☐ My writing makes sense.

BUY THIS ______________________________!

Cut and paste a picture from a magazine or flyer of something you would like to sell. Complete this advertisement to convince people to buy it.

Contact me at:

Selling price:

Let me tell you why!

____

____

____

____

____

____

____

☐ I used capitals and end marks. ☐ My printing is neat. ☐ My writing makes sense.

WANTED!

For: ______________________________

Please call:

Reward:

Who or what? ______________________________

When last seen? ______________________________

Where last seen? ______________________________

Description: ______________________________

☐ I used capitals and end marks. ☐ My printing is neat. ☐ My writing makes sense.

Write a Friendly Letter

____
DATE

Dear ______________________,
GREETING

BODY

____

____

____

____

____

____

____

____

____

____

____

____

____

- ☐ **C**apitalization
- ☐ **O**rganization
- ☐ **P**unctuation
- ☐ **S**pelling

Sincerely,

____
CLOSING / SIGNATURE

Poster Title: ______________________________

Create a poster. What is the purpose of this poster?

☐ to give information ☐ to persuade ☐ to entertain

Social Media Post

Create a fun social media post about something you love!

☐ I used capitals and end marks. ☐ My printing is neat. ☐ My writing makes sense.

Narrative Writing Planner

Narrative writing tells a story that has a beginning, a middle, and an end. It can be about something that actually happened, or it can be made up.

Title: ______________________________

Setting: Where will the story take place?	**Characters:** Who will be in the story?
Problem in the story: What is the problem in the story?	
Events in the story: What happens in the story?	
How the problem is solved: How does the story end?	

Write a Narrative

Title: ______________________________

Beginning

- ☐ I wrote an attention-grabbing first sentence.
- ☐ I introduced the main character(s) and included details.
- ☐ I wrote about where and when the story takes place.

____

____

____

____

____

____

____

____

☐	**Capitalization**	• Do my sentences and proper nouns have capital letters?
☐	**Organization**	• Did I order my ideas in a way that makes sense?
☐	**Punctuation**	• Do my sentences have end marks? (. ! ?)
☐	**Spelling**	• Did I check my spelling to the best of my ability?

Write a Narrative

Problem ☐ I explained the problem in the story.

Events
☐ I wrote about events that happen before the problem is solved.
☐ I told my story in order using the linking words *first, then*, or *next*.
☐ I added details to each event to show what was happening.

Event 1:

☐ **C**apitalization • Do my sentences and proper nouns have capital letters?
☐ **O**rganization • Did I order my ideas in a way that makes sense?
☐ **P**unctuation • Do my sentences have end marks? (. ! ?)
☐ **S**pelling • Did I check my spelling to the best of my ability?

Write a Narrative

Event 2:

____

____

____

____

Ending ☐ I explained how the problem was solved.

Ending:

____

____

____

____

- ☐ **Capitalization** • Do my sentences and proper nouns have capital letters?
- ☐ **Organization** • Did I order my ideas in a way that makes sense?
- ☐ **Punctuation** • Do my sentences have end marks? (. ! ?)
- ☐ **Spelling** • Did I check my spelling to the best of my ability?

Congratulations!

Great Work!

Answers

Consonant Blends pp. 4–5

1. a) flag b) bring c) spider d) scooter e) stick f) clock g) drum h) plant i) skunk j) crafts

2.

S	Q	Y	B	T	V	D	E	L
W	A	U	G	R	A	S	S	F
A	N	T	O	U	F	X	P	E
N	G	Y	E	C	R	H	A	Q
B	L	A	N	K	E	T	C	W
V	O	F	R	E	S	H	E	N
J	V	U	E	P	C	L	A	P
O	E	Z	D	S	M	E	L	L

3. a) green b) snack c) plate d) spin e) trick f) clown

4. a) pl b) fr c) sp

Long Vowel Patterns pp. 6–8

1. a) ai b) ow c) ea d) ay e) ui f) oa g) ea h) ie i) ow j) igh k) ue l) ee

2. a) ea b) oa c) ie d) ow e) ee f) ai g) ay h) igh i) ue j) ee k) ui l) ai

3. a) ee b) ay c) ui d) ie e) ea f) ai g) ow h) ue i) igh j) oa k) ee l) ai

R-controlled Vowels p. 9

1. ir **2.** er **3.** or **4.** ar **5.** ar **6.** ur **7.** er **8.** ir **9.** ur **10.** or **11.** ar **12.** er

What Is a Noun? p. 10

1. Elias, Amy, boy, man, mother, doctor

2. school, library, kitchen, mall, beach, Canada

3. bottle, ruler, sicks, leaf, frog

4. a) pen, apple, bedroom b) teacher, couch c) dog, brother, backyard

5. a) basement b) Juliette, house c) car, school

6. Answers will vary.

What Are Proper Nouns? p. 12

Answers will vary.

Making Nouns Plural p. 13

1. dishes **2.** puppies **3.** bushes **4.** foxes **5.** wishes

Tricky Plural Nouns pp. 14–16

1. a) photos b) potatoes c) tomatoes d) pianos

2. a) The heroes heard echoes in the canyon.
b) Larry sent me videos of potatoes from his garden.

3. a) halves b) scarves c) wolves d) shelves

4. a) The sheriffs stop the thieves from stealing.
b) Leaves blew over the cliffs

5. a) elves b) halves c) wolves d) loaves e) leaves f) shelves g) knives h) lives

6. child → children mouse → mice person → people

Nouns Review p. 17

1. a) table, tree, dog b) doctor, mall c) house, sister, beach

2. Anwers will vary.

3. a) knives b) brushes c) babies d) photos e) books f) feet g) people h) boxes i) leaves j) puppies

Singular Possessive Nouns p. 18

1. a) Julie's b) dog's c) Wyatt's d) man's

2. a) The dog's treats are in the jar. b) The car's front is dented.

More Practice with Possessive Nouns p. 19

1. My jacket's zipper is broken.

2. Please give me the museum's address.

3. Did you find Amy's shoe?

4. The lion's roar is loud!

5. The school's chair is in the hallway.

6. This is my grandmother's apron.

Plural Possessive Nouns p. 20

1. a) brothers' b) aunts' c) birds' d) dogs' e) people's f) men's

Possessive Nouns Review p. 21

1. a) Amy's b) cat's **2.** a) children's b) cousin's

3. a) The men's tools are in the tool box.
b) The animals' enclosures are very large.
c) The people's houses are on this street.
d) My brothers' games are on the shelf.

Pronouns for People p. 22

1. a) She b) They c) them

2. a) He ran in the field with the class.
b) She gave the book to him. c) They hugged us.

Pronouns for Things p. 23

1. a) it b) They c) them d) They

2. a) They gave it to them. b) They are too small for them to pick.
c) They gave them to us.

Possessive Pronouns pp. 24–25

1. a) my b) his c) their d) your e) our f) its

2. Answers will vary.

3. a) Jason watched his favourite movie.
b) We are going over to her house to swim.
c) The Smiths went to the store in their car.
d) Its sheets need to be changed.
e) "Yazan, is it your turn to play the game?" Luca asked.
f) The doctors said, "It is our job to help you feel better."
g) Trudy said, "You can have my last cookie."

More Possessive Pronouns p. 26

1. a) underlined: his, circled: mine b) underlined: her, circled: his
c) underlined: their, circled: ours

2. a) hers b) ours c) theirs d) yours

Pronouns Review p. 27

1. a) They discussed the school's plans.
b) She is going to the store to buy fruit for him.
c) They said goodbye to us.

2. a) it b) They c) them

3. a) underlined: his, circled: it b) underlined: its, circled: his
c) underlined: their, circled: ours

What Is an Adjective? pp. 28–29

1. a) tall, tree b) huge, smile c) lovely, gift d) funny, movie e) big, garden f) fresh, apple g) tiny, kitten h) beautiful, dress i) small, bird j) difficult, puzzle k) bouncy, ball l) long, trip m) cute, puppy n) shiny, coin

2. Answers will vary.

3. a) dirty b) silver c) kind d) scary e) neat f) little, playful

Answers

Adjectives Before Nouns and After Nouns p. 30

1. a) stars, tiny b) amazing, dinner c) forest, scary d) homework, easy e) funny, movie f) challenging, trail g) bread, delicious

2. a) refreshing → water blue → lake
b) happy → children pink → flowers
c) old → man noisy → birds

Adjectives Can Describe How Many p. 31

1. a) two b) five c) eight d) two, one e) soccer, four, first

2. a) several b) many c) few d) some e) most f) all

Using Adjectives to Compare Two Things p. 32

1. nicer, nicest **2.** strong, strongest **3.** rich, richer
4. darker, darkest **5.** calmer, calmest **6.** quick, quickest

Adjectives That Compare More Than Two Things p. 33

1. a) coolest b) tallest

2. a) the fastest b) the loudest c) the largest

3. a) prettiest b) shaggiest

Tricky Adjectives That Compare p. 34

1. a) better, two things b) worse, two things c) most, more than two things d) farthest, more than two things

Adjectives That Use *More* and *Most* to Compare p. 35

1. a) the brightest b) more fun

2. a) more b) the most c) more d) the most e) more f) the most g) the most h) more

Using the Articles *A, An,* and *The* p. 38

1. the **2.** a **3.** an **4.** the **5.** a **6.** an **7.** an, the

Adjectives Review p. 39

1. Answers will vary. **2.** a) two, one b) many
3. a) taller b) the friendliest **4.** a) the b) an c) a

What Is a Verb? p. 40

1. a) eat b) play c) ties d) knits e) build f) opens

2. a) studies, yells, blows b) washes, watches
c) paints, fixes, sings d) listens, reads
e) drives, explores, sends

Verbs: Choosing the Correct Action p. 42

1. eats **2.** yell **3.** toss **4.** love **5.** jog

The Verbs *Be, Do,* and *Have* pp. 43–44

1. a) are b) is **2.** a) does b) do **3.** a) have b) has
4. a) was b) did c) had d) did e) were, was
5. a) had b) did c) was d) had e) were

More Practice with *Be, Do,* and *Have* p. 45

1. a) past b) present c) past d) past e) present f) present g) past

2. a) was b) have c) did d) are e) am f) have

3. a) was b) did c) have d) were e) had f) did

Linking Verbs p. 47

1. a) linking verb, circled b) action verb, underlined c) linking verb, circled d) linking verb, circled e) action verb, underlined

2. a) linking: is; action: hid b) linking: is; action: play
c) linking: was; action: clapped d) linking: are, action: painted
e) linking: was, action: rolled

Spelling Present Tense Verbs p. 48

1. flies **2.** barks **3.** mixes **4.** finishes **5.** scratches **6.** passes **7.** cries **8.** presses

Past Tense Verbs p. 49

1. a) jumped b) played c) escaped d) talked e) laughed f) helped g) cooked h) coughed

2. a) watched b) lived c) brushed

Spelling Past Tense Verbs p. 50

1. a) chopped b) knitted c) stopped

2. a) fried b) tidied c) copied d) hurried

Tricky Past Tense Verbs pp. 51–52

1. a) had b) ate c) said d) fell

2. a) He drives the toy train around the track.
b) We give the dog a treat for behaving well.

3. a) went b) found c) took d) thought

4. a) We know the answer to the riddle.
b) I drink hot chocolate on a cold winter day.

Future Tense Verbs p. 53

1. a) will visit b) will build c) will ride d) will sing

2. a) We will pack our bags for the family roadtrip.
b) He will plant a vegetable garden in the backyard.

Helping Verbs: Present and Future Tenses pp. 54–55

1. a) are b) is s) am d) are

2. a) helping: are, main: learning b) helping: am, main: eating
c) helping: is, main: riding

3. a) My parents will cook dinner in the kitchen. b) I will write a letter to my friend. c) The bus will pick us up at eight o'clock.
d) The students will clean up the classroom.

Helping Verbs: Past Tense p. 56

1. a) has b) had c) was d) have e) were **2.** Answers will vary.
3. a) building b) shining c) riding d) studying
4. a) skipping b) watching c) baking d) writing

Subject–Verb Agreement p. 58

1. a) drive b) finishes c) glow d) teaches e) howls f) skip

2. a) bake b) grows c) fixes d) run e) jump

3. a) takes b) cook c) rushes d) waters e) washes

Pronoun–Verb Agreement pp. 60–61

1. a) read b) practices c) fixes d) give e) knit f) paints

2. a) passes b) buy c) studies d) notice

3. a) keeps, blanket b) twinkle, stars c) buzzes, alarm
d) help, spoons e) goes, belt f) toast, fire

Answers

Verbs Review pp. 62–63

1. a) are b) am c) are d) is

2. a) linking: are; action: playing b) linking: is; action: jogging
c) linking: was; action: baked

3. a) watched b) closed c) baked d) helped

4. a) swim b) studies c) barks

5. a) I will draw a picture in my notebook.
b) They will watch a movie at the theatre.

6. a) has b) had **7.** a) run b) explains **8.** a) carry b) misses

Adverbs Describe How or Where p. 64

1. a) hungrily b) gently c) excitedly d) carefully

2. a) inside b) around c) somewhere

Adverbs Describe When p. 65

1. a) on sunny days b) sometimes c) before dinner
d) on weekends e) every Tuesday

2. a) soon, fall b) next, plays

Adverbs Describe How Often p. 66

1. a) twice b) usually c) rarely

2. a) frequently b) constantly c) rarely d) usually

Adverbs Review p. 67

1. a) slowly b) quickly c) excitedly
2. a) inside b) outside c) over there
3. a) at night, reads b) today, riding
4. a) frequently b) occasionally

Complete Subjects p. 68

1. The shiny ladybug **2.** Several outgoing students

3. The waves of the ocean **4.** Many smart scientists

5. The playful otter **6.** My older brother Dylan **7.** A lot of kids in my neighbourhood

Complete Predicates p. 69

1. hung from the branches of the tree

2. floated in the air at the birthday party

3. delivered letters to every house on the street

4. chased each other around the living room

5. plowed the farmer's fields **6.** worked hard to build a new road

7. played a game of tag in the park

What Comes at the End of a Sentence? pp. 70–71

1. to 4. Answers will vary.

5. a) ? b) ! c) . d) ? e) ! f) . g) ?

One Sentence or Two? p. 72

1. The bird built a nest. It was made of twigs.

2. It was windy. I lost my hat.

3. Jack loves to swim. He dives into the pool.

4. The teacher gave us homework. It was hard.

5. The doorbell rang. It was my friend Ali.

Joining Sentences with *And* or *But* p. 73

1. a) but b) and **2.** a) but b) and c) but

Joining Sentences with *Or* or *So* p. 74

1. a) or b) so **2.** a) or b) so c) or

Sentences and Punctuation Review p. 75

1. a) The four cheesy pizzas b) The tall funny clown

2. a) splashed everywhere when he jumped in the pool
b) finished their science homework before recess

3. a) He finished his homework. He felt proud.
b) The dog barked loudly. It scared me.

4. a) and b) but **5.** a) so b) or

What Is a Contraction? p. 76

1. a) they're b) I'm c) We're d) you're

2. a) She's so happy that it's summer vacation next week.
b) I'm feeling tired, but that's not going to stop me!

More Contractions p. 77

1. a) We'll b) you'll c) he'll d) I'll

2. a) I will help you with math and you will help me with science. We will both do great!

Abbreviations p. 78

1. a) Dr. b) road c) St. d) avenue e) Mr. f) doctor, Rd.

2. a) Dr. Watson is best friends with Mr. Harris.
b) River Ave. is near Storybook St.

Contractions and Abbreviations Review p. 79

1. a) I'll wait for you, but we're leaving soon.
b) You're moving to a new city, and that's why I'm sad.

2. We will have to hurry if we are going to catch the bus before it is too late!

3. a) Dr. b) Mr. c) street d) Ave. e) road, Rd.

Homophones p. 80

1. blue, blew **2.** meet, meat **3.** write, right **4.** their, there

5. two, too **6.** week, weak

Homophones: *There, Their,* and *They're* p. 81

1. there **2.** their **3.** they're **4.** their **5.** there **6.** they're

7. there **8.** They're **9.** their

Synonyms and Antonyms p. 82

1. b **2.** b **3.** a **4.** b **5.** a

6.

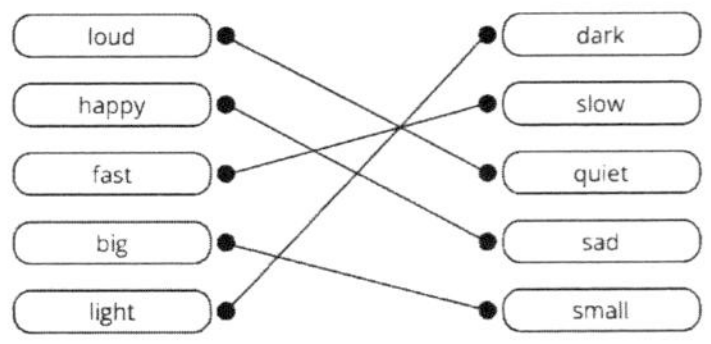

Synonym, Antonym, and Homophone Review p. 83

1. a) ate, eight b) there, their c) bye, buy

2. Answers will vary. **3.** Answers will vary.

Answers

Context Clues pp. 84–85

1. b **2.** c **3.** a **4.** c **5.** b **6.** c **7.** b **8.** c **9.** b **10.** c **11.** a **12.** b **13.** a **14.** c **15.** c **16.** a

We Need a Class Pet pp. 86–89

1. a **2.** b **3. to 6.** Answers will vary.

Birds and Bats pp. 90–93

1. c **2.** Only birds: have feathers, lays eggs Only bats: active at night, babies drink milk, sleep upside down Birds and bats: have wings, help farmers **3.** d **4.** Animals that sleep during the day and are active at night. **5.** Answers will vary.

6.

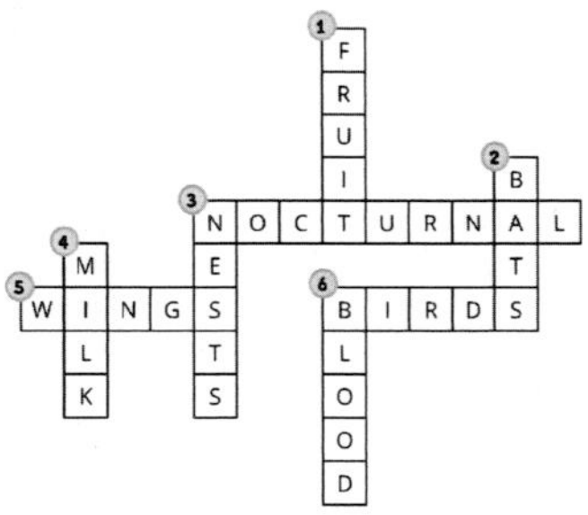

Mouse and Lion pp. 94–97

1. b **2.** c **3.** c **4.** a **5.** c **6.** b

7. Answers will vary. Sample: Because mouse wanted to be let go.

8. Answers will vary. Sample: Her teeth will be able to chew through the rope.

9. Answers will vary. Sample: Not to underestimate someone just because they're smaller than you.

10. Answers will vary.

The World's Tallest Animal pp. 98–101

1. a **2.** b **3.** c **4.** c **5. and 6.** Answers will vary.

My Super Racecar pp. 102–105

1. b **2.** a, c

3.

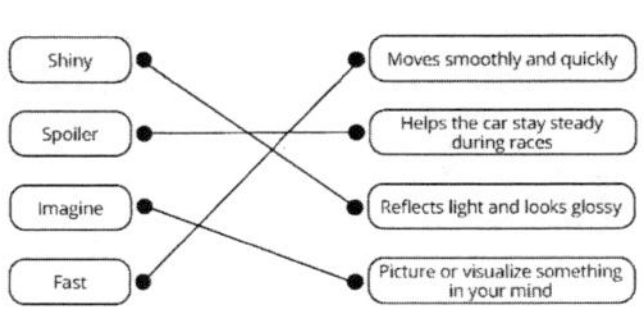

4. a) T b) F c) F d) F e) T

5. Appearance: big, bright, cool, round, shiny, silver, sleek
Texture: smooth Speed: fast

6. Answers will vary

My Morning Routine pp. 106–109

1. a **2.** 1 4 2 6 3 7 5

3. Sample answers: bathroom, breakfast, notebooks, backpack

4. Answers will vary. **5.** d

6. a) Next, I head to the kitchen for breakfast.
b) Sometimes, I have toast with jam, too.
c) First, I put my books and notebooks inside it.
d) I wake up and stretch my arms and legs.

7. Answers will vary.

Dad's Birthday pp. 110–113

1. a **2.** c **3.** four **4.** a) cause b) effect

5. Both parties: Liam made something for Dad, Dad gets a red sweater
Only the surprise party: is not on his birthday, is a big party

6. Liam's Mom - "We'll have the party on Saturday to make sure he's surprised." Liam's Dad - "Sometimes grownups get a tear or two when they are very happy."

7. and 8. Answers will vary.

Wolves and Dogs pp. 114–117

1. Dogs: like to be around people, usually bark Wolves: all have the same eye colour, don't like to be near people Both: have more than one baby at a time, adults have 42 teeth

2. c

3.

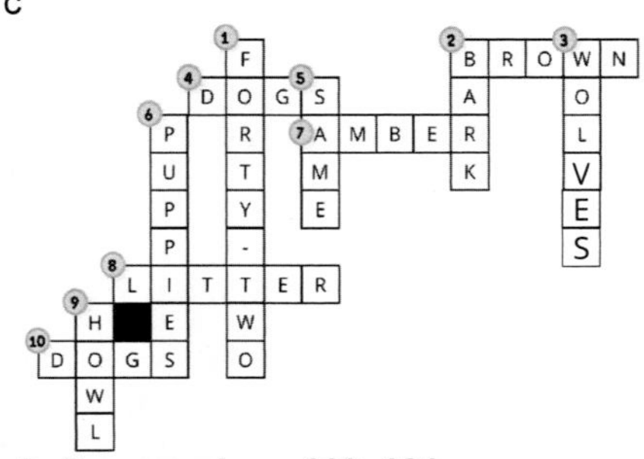

4. Answers will vary.

Viola Desmond pp. 118–121

1. c **2.** a **3.** c **4.** b **5.** b **6.** Answers will vary.

7. a) T b) F c) T d) F e) F **8.** Answers will vary.

Making Cheese pp. 122–125

1. b **2.** a **3.** b **4.** c **5.** c

6. 4 2
3 5
1 6

7. b **8.** a) fresh b) cream c) cultures, curds d) cubes e) salt f) butter

9. a) swiss b) parmesan c) brie d) gouda e) feta f) ricotta

10. to 12. Answers will vary.

Spiders pp. 126–129

1.

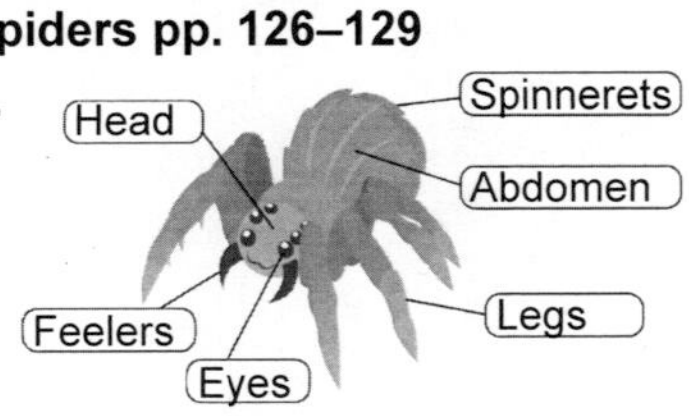

2. forests

3. a) effect b) cause

4. b **5.** b **6.** c **7.** a **8.** Answers will vary.

The Leaf Project pp. 130–133

1. b) **2.**

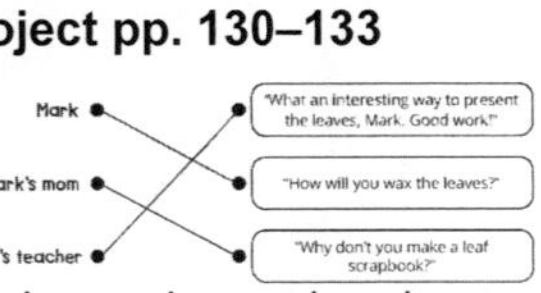

3. a) F b) F c) F d) O e) F

4. Sample: oak, maple, poplar, dogwood, willow, beech

5. c **6.** a) effect b) cause **7.** a) willow b) beech

8. Answers will vary.

Arctic and Antarctic pp. 134–137

1. a **2.** a) effect b) cause **3.** winter **4.** Sample answer: caribou, Arctic foxes, polar bears, seals **5.** penguins, seals

6. Arctic: a few plants grow during summer, no penguins live there

Answers

Antarctic: penguins live there, is winter in June

7. 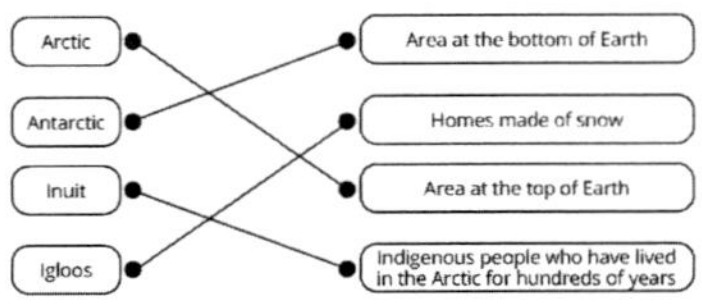

8. a) T b) T c) F d) T
9. Answers will vary.

Inside an Animal Shelter pp. 138–141

1. a **2.** b **3.** find **4.** b **5.** a) T b) F c) T d) F
6. Answers will vary. **7.** a **8.** Answers will vary.

Mighty Moose vs. Terrific Tigers pp. 142–145

1. b **2.** 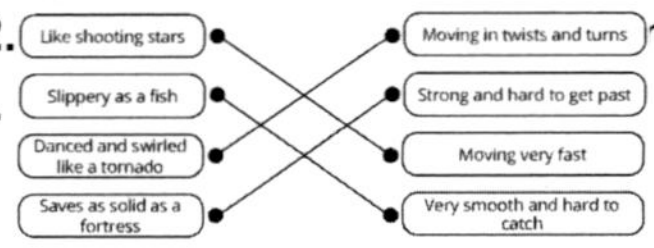 nswers will vary.

7. a **8.**

9. and 10. Answers will vary.

The Eiffel Tower pp. 146–149

1. d) **2.** five **3.** a) effect b) cause
4. Top: narrowest part, must use an elevator to get there
Bottom: widest part, use stairs or elevator to go up
5. a) T b) F c) T d) T f) T g) T h) T i) F j) T
6. Answers will vary.

Three Kinds of Bees pp. 150–153

1. colony **2.** c **3.** b **4.** a **5.** Answers will vary.
6. Queen bees: lay eggs, largest bees Worker bees: contro temperature, collect nectar and pollen, thousands in a colony, feed the queen bee Drones: all male, no stingers, are mates for the queen, hundreds in a colony
7. Answers will vary.

Convincing People to Buy a Product pp. 154–157

1. c **2.** Advertising tries to convince people to buy the product that is advertised. **3.** a **4.** b **5.** b **6.** a) fact b) opinion c) opinion d) fact **7. to 9.** Answers will vary.

Amazing Stories pp. 158–161

1. b **2.** a) T b) F c) F d) F e) T
3. 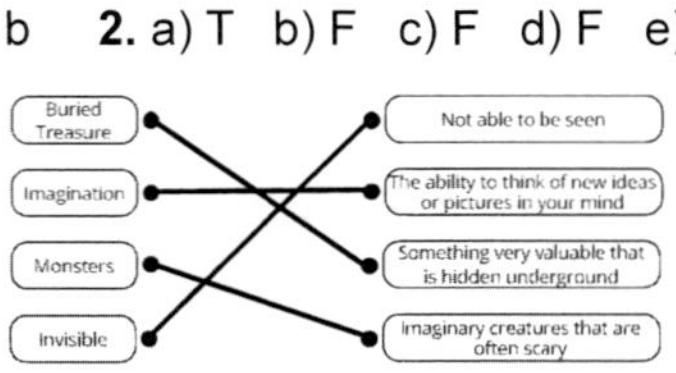

4. a) ✓ b) ✓ c) ×

5. A girl gets a toy robot for her birthday, her cat climbs onto her desk
6. She gets the robot to do her homework for her, her cat speaks
7. Answers will vary.

David Suzuki pp. 162–165

1. a **2.** b **3.** a **4.** c **5.** c **6.** Answers will vary.

7. 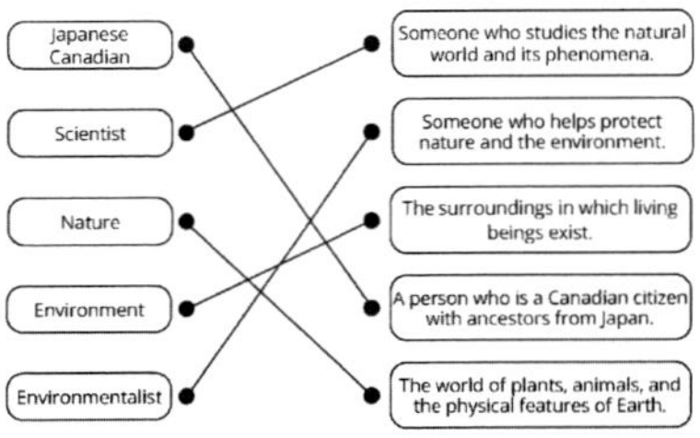

8. 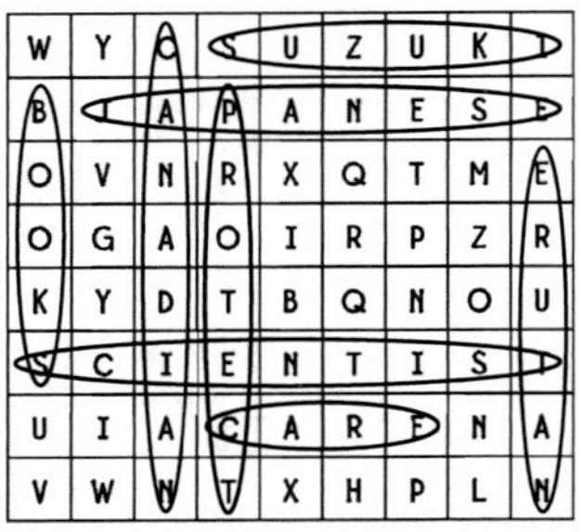

9. Answers will vary.

Fluffy pp. 166–169

1. c **2.** b **3.** c **4.** a **5.** c
6. Physical traits: snow-white fur, long ears, big round blue eyes, small round body, four little paws, tiny claws, pink nose, always sniffing for treats,
Personality traits: never scratches, loves to nap, plays with her ball, loves to hop around the yard, loves the dew, when happy does a hop and twist in the air called a "binky," nudges your leg with her nose when she wants attention
7. Answers will vary.

Johnny's Magical Adventures pp. 170–173

1. a) giant b) lion c) kangaroo d) magic e) wide f) feats g) breeze h) laugh
2. Sample: With a leap as high as a kangaroo, a heart as wild as a stampeding herd of horses, roared like a lion
3. and 4. Answers will vary.

Cree Powwow pp. 174–177

1. 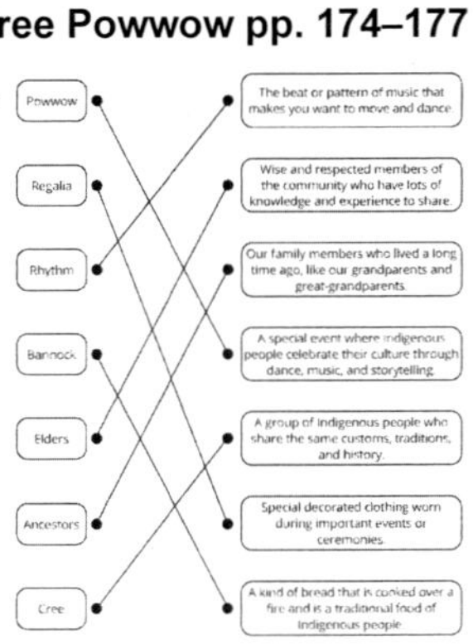

2. a **3.** c **4.** d **5.** b **6.** b
7. Answers will vary.